MAGGIE HELEN is an experienced counsellor and trainer and is currently employed as Policy Development Officer with a national charity. She was the Client Services Manager for an Alcohol and Drugs Advisory Service and has worked as a counsellor for Cruse Bereavement Care. She is a member of the International Association for Counselling and the Association for Death Education and Counseling. She was ten when her mother took her own life following a prolonged illness. She lives with her partner in the West Country.

Overcoming Common Problems Series

For a full list of titles please contact
Sheldon Press, Marylebone Road, London NW1 4DU

Antioxidants
Dr Robert Youngson

The Assertiveness Workbook
Joanna Gutmann

Beating the Comfort Trap
Dr Windy Dryden and Jack Gordon

Body Language
Allan Pease

Body Language in Relationships
David Cohen

Calm Down
Dr Paul Hauck

Cancer – A Family Affair
Neville Shone

The Cancer Guide for Men
Helen Beare and Neil Priddy

The Candida Diet Book
Karen Brody

Caring for Your Elderly Parent
Julia Burton-Jones

Cider Vinegar
Margaret Hills

Comfort for Depression
Janet Horwood

Considering Adoption?
Sarah Biggs

Coping Successfully with Hay Fever
Dr Robert Youngson

Coping Successfully with Pain
Neville Shone

Coping Successfully with Panic Attacks
Shirley Trickett

Coping Successfully with PMS
Karen Evennett

Coping Successfully with Prostate Problems
Rosy Reynolds

Coping Successfully with RSI
Maggie Black and Penny Gray

Coping Successfully with Your Hiatus Hernia
Dr Tom Smith

Coping Successfully with Your Irritable Bladder
Dr Jennifer Hunt

Coping Successfully with Your Irritable Bowel
Rosemary Nicol

Coping When Your Child Has Special Needs
Suzanne Askham

Coping with Anxiety and Depression
Shirley Trickett

Coping with Blushing
Dr Robert Edelmann

Coping with Bronchitis and Emphysema
Dr Tom Smith

Coping with Candida
Shirley Trickett

Coping with Chronic Fatigue
Trudie Chalder

Coping with Coeliac Disease
Karen Brody

Coping with Cystitis
Caroline Clayton

Coping with Depression and Elation
Dr Patrick McKeon

Coping with Eczema
Dr Robert Youngson

Coping with Endometriosis
Jo Mears

Coping with Epilepsy
Fiona Marshall and
Dr Pamela Crawford

Coping with Fibroids
Mary-Claire Mason

Coping with Gallstones
Dr Joan Gomez

Coping with Headaches and Migraine
Shirley Trickett

Coping with a Hernia
Dr David Delvin

Coping with Long-Term Illness
Barbara Baker

Coping with the Menopause
Janet Horwood

Coping with Psoriasis
Professor Ronald Marks

Coping with Rheumatism and Arthritis
Dr Robert Youngson

Overcoming Common Problems Series

Coping with Stammering
Trudy Stewart and Jackie Turnbull

Coping with Stomach Ulcers
Dr Tom Smith

Coping with Strokes
Dr Tom Smith

Coping with Thrush
Caroline Clayton

Coping with Thyroid Problems
Dr Joan Gomez

Curing Arthritis – The Drug-Free Way
Margaret Hills

**Curing Arthritis – More ways to a
drug-free life**
Margaret Hills

Curing Arthritis Diet Book
Margaret Hills

Curing Arthritis Exercise Book
Margaret Hills and Janet Horwood

Cystic Fibrosis – A Family Affair
Jane Chumbley

Depression
Dr Paul Hauck

Depression at Work
Vicky Maud

**Everything Parents Should Know
About Drugs**
Sarah Lawson

Fertility
Julie Reid

Feverfew
Dr Stewart Johnson

Gambling – A Family Affair
Angela Willans

Garlic
Karen Evennett

Getting a Good Night's Sleep
Fiona Johnston

The Good Stress Guide
Mary Hartley

Heart Attacks – Prevent and Survive
Dr Tom Smith

**Helping Children Cope with Attention
Deficit Disorder**
Dr Patricia Gilbert

Helping Children Cope with Bullying
Sarah Lawson

Helping Children Cope with Divorce
Rosemary Wells

Helping Children Cope with Grief
Rosemary Wells

Helping Children Cope with Stammering
Jackie Turnbull and Trudy Stewart

Hold Your Head Up High
Dr Paul Hauck

How to Accept Yourself
Dr Windy Dryden

How to Be Your Own Best Friend
Dr Paul Hauck

How to Cope when the Going Gets Tough
Dr Windy Dryden and Jack Gordon

How to Cope with Anaemia
Dr Joan Gomez

How to Cope with Bulimia
Dr Joan Gomez

How to Cope with Difficult Parents
Dr Windy Dryden and Jack Gordon

How to Cope with Difficult People
Alan Houel with Christian Godefroy

**How to Cope with People who Drive
You Crazy**
Dr Paul Hauck

How to Cope with Stress
Dr Peter Tyrer

How to Enjoy Your Retirement
Vicky Maud

How to Get Where You Want to Be
Christian Godefroy

How to Improve Your Confidence
Dr Kenneth Hambly

How to Interview and Be Interviewed
Michele Brown and Gyles Brandreth

How to Keep Your Cholesterol in Check
Dr Robert Povey

How to Lose Weight Without Dieting
Mark Barker

How to Love and Be Loved
Dr Paul Hauck

How to Pass Your Driving Test
Donald Ridland

How to Raise Confident Children
Carole Baldock

How to Stand up for Yourself
Dr Paul Hauck

**How to Start a Conversation and Make
Friends**
Don Gabor

Overcoming Common Problems Series

How to Stick to a Diet
Deborah Steinberg and Dr Windy Dryden

How to Stop Worrying
Dr Frank Tallis

The How to Study Book
Alan Brown

How to Succeed as a Single Parent
Carole Baldock

How to Untangle Your Emotional Knots
Dr Windy Dryden and Jack Gordon

How to Write a Successful CV
Joanna Gutmann

Hysterectomy
Suzie Hayman

The Irritable Bowel Diet Book
Rosemary Nicol

The Irritable Bowel Stress Book
Rosemary Nicol

Is HRT Right for You?
Dr Anne MacGregor

Jealousy
Dr Paul Hauck

Living with Asthma
Dr Robert Youngson

Living with Crohn's Disease
Dr Joan Gomez

Living with Diabetes
Dr Joan Gomez

Living with Fibromyalgia
Christine Craggs-Hinton

Living with Grief
Dr Tony Lake

Living with High Blood Pressure
Dr Tom Smith

Living with Nut Allergies
Karen Evennett

Living with Osteoporosis
Dr Joan Gomez

Living with a Stoma
Dr Craig White

Making Friends with Your Stepchildren
Rosemary Wells

Motor Neurone Disease – A Family Affair
Dr David Oliver

Overcoming Anger
Dr Windy Dryden

Overcoming Anxiety
Dr Windy Dryden

Overcoming Guilt
Dr Windy Dryden

Overcoming Jealousy
Dr Windy Dryden

Overcoming Procrastination
Dr Windy Dryden

Overcoming Shame
Dr Windy Dryden

Overcoming Your Addictions
Dr Windy Dryden and
Dr Walter Matweychuk

The Parkinson's Disease Handbook
Dr Richard Godwin-Austen

The PMS Diet Book
Karen Evennett

A Positive Thought for Every Day
Dr Windy Dryden

Rheumatoid Arthritis
Mary-Claire Mason and Dr Elaine Smith

Second Time Around
Anne Lovell

Serious Mental Illness – A Family Affair
Gwen Howe

Shift Your Thinking, Change Your Life
Mo Shapiro

The Stress Workbook
Joanna Gutmann

The Subfertility Handbook
Virginia Ironside and Sarah Biggs

Successful Au Pairs
Hilli Matthews

Talking with Confidence
Don Gabor

Ten Steps to Positive Living
Dr Windy Dryden

Think Your Way to Happiness
Dr Windy Dryden and Jack Gordon

The Travellers' Good Health Guide
Ted Lankester

Understanding Obsessions and Compulsions
Dr Frank Tallis

Understanding Sex and Relationships
Rosemary Stones

Understanding Your Personality
Patricia Hedges

Work–Life Balance
Gordon and Ronni Lamont

Overcoming Common Problems

Coping with Suicide

Maggie Helen

sheldon PRESS

First published in Great Britain in 2002 by
Sheldon Press
1 Marylebone Road
London NW1 4DU

British Library Cataloguing-in-Publication Data

A catalogue record for this book is available from the British Library

ISBN 0–85969–871–8

Typeset by Deltatype Limited, Birkenhead, Merseyside
Printed in Great Britain by Biddles Ltd
www.biddles.co.uk

Contents

Acknowledgements ix

Foreword xi

Introduction xiii

1 The Faces of Suicide 1

2 Confronting the Truth 9

3 Suicidal Risk 18

4 Youth Suicide 27

5 Seeking Understanding 37

6 Practical Concerns 47

7 The Impact of Suicide 59

8 A Special Grief 73

9 Finding Support 85

10 Shaping the Future 95

Further Reading 105

Useful Addresses 106

Index 111

Acknowledgements

I would like to thank all the people who have so willingly shared their experiences with me over the past months and hope I have accurately represented their views and feelings. A special thank you to my partner, Jonathan, for his patient reviewing of the material and his continuing support.

I dedicate this book to my mother. Although I didn't have the chance to get to know her, I still draw hope and courage from her memory.

Foreword

Written with a deep compassion and personal understanding of the anguish left behind after a suicide death, Maggie Helen comprehensively covers the trauma that follows a suicide bereavement and leads a very structured and thorough approach through the pain and anguish of people left behind.

Maggie understands the problems of the suicide bereaved and has an appreciation of the human issues. As well as experiencing suicide bereavement herself first hand, she has interviewed other survivors and also people who have attempted suicide themselves.

She deals with adjustment sensitively, and covers the complexity of postmortems, the minefields of inquests, the media, and insensitivity from well-meaning friends and colleagues.

Drawing to a close with survival strategies and resources available, suggesting how survivors may be helped along the tragic path they have to tread, she offers hope and assurance that the survivor will cope with this devastating bereavement.

Her book will be invaluable to all survivors of bereavement by suicide and also to professionals in this field.

Survivors of Bereavement by Suicide

Introduction

When someone takes their own life, we may think about the missed opportunities and wasted potential of the individual. A suicide can be equally shocking whether it happens to someone young or to someone old. Their reasons for suicide may be very different, but what the individuals probably had in common was the feeling that they had no future to look forward to. Those left behind, though, now have their own future to face.

Each completed act of suicide leaves an estimated five to eight people significantly affected by the death. In addition to family and friends, these may include witnesses to the act, the person who finds the body, colleagues and neighbours. The frequent perception of suicide as a socially unacceptable way to die means that support can sometimes be difficult to find.

Suicide hurts close family members, partners and friends most deeply. This book addresses those 'suicide survivors' who are left behind when a loved one takes his or her own life. *Coping with Suicide* offers an insight into the unique nature of the survivors' grief as they begin the journey from despair to emotional recovery. The book encourages an active and positive approach in coming to terms with this devastating loss, and acknowledging the responsibility we carry for our own happiness. Friends and practitioners offering help and guidance to those bereaved by suicide may also find the information useful.

Important note

This book is written in good faith as a self-help guide. Ideas and suggestions are intended to complement professional medical advice or supervision rather than be a substitute for them. Individuals with a medical condition should consult their doctor or a specialist therapist.

1
The Faces of Suicide

Suicide is the act of intentional self-killing. The deliberate nature of the act is likely both to alarm and threaten us, as it seems to go against our ideas about the importance of the preservation of life. Rates of suicide and attempted suicide continue to rise and, although there are known risk factors, the phenomenon cuts across social, cultural and economic boundaries. Suicide occurs in all kinds of families – whether large or small, rich or poor, organized or chaotic. There is no single cause and individual motives can be elusive; therefore every suicide has its own story.

Incidence and trends

Suicide affects not just the family and friends of the individual, but the wider community. In the last 45 years, the rates worldwide have increased by an astounding 60 per cent, and it has become an important public health concern in many countries. Suicide is now among the three leading causes of loss of life among 15 to 44-year-olds. The United Kingdom records around 6,000 suicides annually – this figure equates to twice the number of fatalities caused by road traffic accidents. Rates have been rising steadily, particularly in Europe, Australia, New Zealand, the United States and Canada, and in Ireland suicide is now the leading cause of death in young people. The World Health Organization estimates that one million people worldwide are dying from suicide each year.

For a suicide to be recorded as such it must be clear that the person intended to take their own life. However, there may be a lack of evidence, and sometimes there is an understandable reluctance on the part of the family and the medical profession to admit that an individual died through suicide. Consequently, many coroners record an open verdict, which means that no conclusion can be drawn, or an accidental death. Some estimates put the suicide rate at least 50–60 per cent higher than the official figures. On an international basis, under-reporting is common, partly because there's no agreed

1

definition of suicide to assist in gathering information. In addition, self-killing is a highly sensitive issue in countries where there are cultural sanctions, and some Arab and Latin American countries, for example, record few or no deaths from suicide.

Attempted suicide and self-harm

A suicide attempt that results in death is termed 'successful' or 'completed'. Fortunately, only a small proportion of attempts end in death. Non-fatal acts are referred to as attempted suicide, parasuicide or deliberate self-harm. Completed and non-fatal suicide differ in the methods adopted and predisposing factors. Women more frequently make attempts on their lives, although completed suicide is more common in men. There are around 200,000 attempts reported annually in the United Kingdom and the incidence is rising, particularly among young women. This figure comes from statistics from emergency departments and hospital admissions only, so doesn't take into account those the doctor sees in the surgery or on home visits.

Self-harming behaviour can become entrenched as a strategy for coping with frustrating situations and physical or emotional pain. Common suicide gestures include slashing or wounding the body and non-lethal overdose. We often perceive acts of deliberate self-harm as a cry for help. This view, however, may prevent us from addressing what is clearly very disturbed behaviour, especially if it recurs. There is always a risk that acts of deliberate self-harm will lead to eventual death.

Sometimes a suicidal person will feel ambivalent about their life and may leave it to fate as to whether a risk they take ends in death. Some of them, like Hannah, are literally gambling with their lives:

Hannah is in her late twenties, suffers from bouts of depression and has made two previous suicide attempts. 'The last time I took a drug overdose, I really didn't care if I lived or died. Now, I wish I'd succeeded because my life's so miserable.' Hannah is attending therapy sessions to address her depression, although she admits she is still vulnerable to making a further suicide attempt.

2

Accident or design?

It's not always certain whether a death is the result of suicide or an accident. If the evidence is ambiguous, the coroner normally classifies the death as accidental or undetermined. Sadly, for those of us left behind, this means that our loved ones take their secrets with them, leaving us to guess what happened. If you were close to the person who has died, this can feel like a profound betrayal of the relationship you once shared. In the absence of a suicide note, to prove a calculated rather than an accidental overdose, for instance, can be very difficult. Other uncertain deaths include car crashes where no other vehicles are involved, drowning, or 'mishaps' with guns.

Jamila's father died when his car piled into a motorway bridge early on a Sunday morning. Jamila said, 'He wrote me a strange letter about three weeks before the crash, saying how much he missed my mother since the divorce. I think he was severely depressed, but he'd never admit it. That's what makes me think it was intentional, and that he really wanted to die. I'll never be absolutely sure and that's very hard to live with.' The coroner recorded death by misadventure.

It's perhaps inevitable that young people flirt with risky or self-destructive behaviour while they're learning to stretch their wings. Thankfully, they usually maintain some boundaries and withdraw before an activity becomes too dangerous. Sometimes, though, they do push the limits – particularly under the influence of drink or drugs. Such a risk might go tragically wrong, ending in a death that could look like a suicide.

Types of suicide

Intentional suicide
The type of suicide we most frequently hear about is one in which the individual seeks relief from unbearable problems in his or her life. People may carry out the suicide when they're in a state of extreme stress, or disorientation. Many of us experience suicidal

3

thoughts at some time in our lives. Normally these subside when we see alternative solutions or an end to our emotional pain.

Manipulation

The motive for suicide might be an attempt to make you, the survivor, feel sad, ashamed or guilty about something, and it's very easy to respond by regretting things you've said or done. There's no way of knowing whether your loved one was conscious of their motive or intended their death to have this effect on you. Whatever you believe about their reasons for suicide, you need to remember that you can only have an impact on some aspects of a person's life. Most influences are out of your control, and so it isn't realistic to feel responsible for your loved one's actions.

In a suicide threat that has an element of coercion attached, the individual is clearly hoping to influence your behaviour. So, when someone says, 'I'll kill myself if you leave me', or, 'If I take an overdose, it'll be all your fault', they're implying that you are entirely responsible for their actions. The person may be feeling very desperate and in need of help, and this is the only way they can express their frustration or unhappiness. You must not, however, accept such an unfair burden of responsibility and it can put you in an impossible situation. Those who do, often find that the threats continue and their position is increasingly compromised.

Martyrs

A martyr sacrifices his or her own life for a cause or ideal that they perceive as greater than the self. Examples range from the Japanese samurai warrior carrying out ritual suicide to present-day suicide bombers or hunger strikers with a political or religious conviction or intent.

Mass suicide

Cases of mass suicide are often associated with spiritual cults and sects that have a powerful or charismatic leader. Followers believe the individual can lead them to transformation, or to a higher spiritual plane, through death. In 1997 in California, 39 members of the Higher Source cult died after a mass suicide. In the year 2000 in Uganda, up to 470 people belonging to the Restoration of the Ten Commandments sect burned themselves to death by barricading themselves inside a blazing church.

4

THE FACES OF SUICIDE

Non-conventional suicide

Non-conventional suicide describes certain forms of self-destructive behaviour. A proportion of individuals walk a slow yet deliberate path to personal annihilation. They might hasten their own death through chronic alcohol or drug use, take unnecessary risks with their health, or shun life-saving treatment.

Rational suicide

A trend in Western societies acknowledges suicide as a rational alternative to life, especially for those suffering from mental or physical ill health. Some would argue that there's no such thing as rational suicide. This view proposes that anyone who takes the crucial decision to die must be suffering from a distorted perspective, so the decision is always irrational.

After illness

Many people with a chronic or terminal illness face the prospect of a declining quality of life. Some, like my own mum, choose to kill themselves in preference to allowing nature to take its painful course. Society tends to regard the motivation for this type of suicide as more acceptable than for others, so we're inclined to show increased tolerance towards it.

> Tom's wife was in her seventies when she killed herself with a massive overdose of painkillers and brandy. Tom said of his wife's decision, 'I know it was what she wanted. Suicide has a different meaning for me now. My wife hated losing her independence and the pain of her rheumatism had accelerated over the last three years. It didn't strike me as being the act of a defeated or crazed woman, but a reasoned way for her to regain peace and dignity.'

My mum died when I was ten years old. She worked as a staff nurse at a psychiatric hospital and she was acutely aware of the implications of her aggressive and inoperable brain tumour. Mum suffered a deterioration in her mental and physical health, which included recurring fits and severe depression. Her job gave her access to drugs, and the decision to take her life was intentional and planned well in advance. I'm sure that to leave my dad, my brother and me must have been the most tormented decision she ever made. I'm heartbroken that she needed to escape from her frightening and distressing existence, but I've never doubted her wisdom or her right to make this final choice.

It isn't always easy for those left behind to regard suicide as the only option their loved one had. Although it might have been a planned decision to end suffering, the effect on the survivors is still devastating and some find it hard to forgive. As one young man said after his father's suicide, 'He was going to die in a few months anyway. I'd have nursed him so he died in peace. I felt as though he'd deprived me of his final days and the chance to say goodbye.'

A number of high-profile suicide pacts carried out by elderly couples have left their adult children feeling resentful about losing both their parents at the same time. This is understandable, particularly if only one parent was suffering from a painful or terminal illness and the other had agreed to die with them.

Physician-assisted suicide

Despite medication and techniques for managing pain, a significant number of patients still endure terrible physical or mental agony, with little or no prospect of recovery. Physician-assisted suicide, sometimes known as euthanasia, involves doctors in administering lethal drugs to terminally ill patients who are asking to end their lives. The practice is illegal in most countries. Switzerland and Belgium tolerate euthanasia, and the Netherlands passed a Voluntary Euthanasia Bill in 2001. The state of Oregon is the only one in the United States that has actually legalized physician-assisted suicide. Numerous moral, emotional and legal issues underlie the assisted-suicide debate, but these are problems we need to face up to in order to retain our humanity and compassion for those in intolerable pain.

Attitudes to suicide

The perception of suicide has varied over time and in different societies and cultures. Many societies endeavour to protect individuals from harming themselves as well as one another. Popular culture

6

sometimes portrays the act as romantic, melodramatic, decisive or fearless. These images can be seductive to certain people. Indeed, some of us might find it appealing to challenge death head on, rather than waiting for it to steal up on us when we least expect it.

Until the Suicide Act of 1961, the United Kingdom treated suicide as 'self-murder' and therefore a criminal offence. It was the last European country to repeal the legislation, and unfortunately some negative perceptions of self-killing still linger on. Even the term 'commit suicide', which is commonly used, can remind us of the historical criminal connotations of the act.

The way others react to suicide tends to differ according to the type of suicide and the apparent motivations of the person. People sometimes judge it a selfish and thoughtless act, because of the immeasurable punishment it can inflict on family and friends. It's often hard, though, for survivors to cope with the accusation that the suicide was self-centred. Comments such as, 'She didn't think of anyone but herself' or 'He never considered what this would do to his parents' are hurtful and may also be wildly inaccurate. This type of judgement is hard for people to make when they can't really know what the individual's life was like or what was going through their mind at the time. That they took such an extreme action as suicide implies they felt desperate and that they'd come to the end of their resources in solving their problems. It's entirely possible that they just couldn't see a way out.

Religious belief

All the major spiritual and religious traditions struggle with the ethics and morality of people taking their own lives. In Catholicism, suicide was the unpardonable sin. Islam, Hinduism, Buddhism and Judaism disapprove of suicide in most situations. The attitude and approach of Christianity, however, seems to have softened in recent years. The condemnation of suicide as 'self-murder' led in the past to the refusal to bury the deceased in consecrated ground, which must have caused untold distress to many families. For those survivors who hold religious beliefs that condemn suicide, the fact that a loved one has taken their own life will quite possibly provoke strong feelings of discomfort, anger and guilt. Now that the person

7

THE FACES OF SUICIDE

has died, though, it is better to be compassionate and remember how they lived, rather than allowing yourself to dwell on the significance of the manner of their death.

Summary

- It is virtually impossible to collate accurate statistics on suicide owing to under-reporting. Nevertheless, the rates have increased worldwide over recent years.
- More men 'complete' suicide than women, but women make more attempts on their lives.
- There are negative attitudes associated with suicide, although these have varied over time and within different cultures and religions.
- The beliefs of society, friends and family have a considerable effect on those left behind after a loved one's suicide.
- The motivation for suicide varies depending on the type of act.
- The ethical debate on physician-assisted suicide hinges on principles of self-determination and mercy on the one side, and the sanctity of life on the other.

2

Confronting the Truth

Suicide is a trauma that sends shockwaves through a wide circle of people including family, friends, colleagues and neighbours. The death is also distressing for the person finding the body, the police and medical staff. Sometimes a stranger becomes incidentally involved, for example a train driver, when the victim has jumped on to a railtrack.

When someone we love takes their own life the finality of the act can plunge us into a living hell. The questions flood in, but we find them too painful to contemplate. Why did they do it? Where did we go wrong? We may be tempted to look for an outside influence to blame, such as friends, society or alcohol, rather than daring to recognize any troubles within the family. If we embrace our fears and square up to the facts rather than allow fantasy to cloud our understanding, we can begin to deal with the aftermath.

Witness to the act

Although the majority of completed suicides are solitary acts, some people choose to kill themselves in the presence of one or more witnesses.

> Matthew was in the same room when his 22-year-old brother shot himself in the head after a bitter argument with his girlfriend. Matthew was so appalled that he was unable to talk about what happened for months: 'The experience was too overwhelming to take in. It was unreal, like a dream. I watched in horror as he put the gun to his head. I thought he was messing about and I laughed. Blood and pieces of his brain exploded everywhere. Although I've started to recover now, I'll never forget that moment and the sickening feeling in my stomach.'

In the public arena, individuals jump from bridges and buildings, drown themselves, or step into the path of high-speed vehicles. Any number of people may observe the suicide, including truck drivers, motorists, passengers, holidaymakers and passers-by. In the United Kingdom and United States, a significant proportion of self-destructive acts involve people leaping out in front of a train or standing or lying on a railtrack. The train driver may just have time to see the victim, but can do nothing to avoid the impact. Drivers implicated in this shocking way may be tormented by the question of why it should happen to them. Despite the fact that there was no time to prevent the disaster, they may feel a sense of responsibility that has an impact on their lives for many years to come.

The shock of discovery

Debbie walked in on the death scene of her partner, Brendan:

> I had no understanding of suicide except from media reports about famous people overdosing on drugs. I'd always viewed it from a safe distance and didn't consider that it would ever affect my life. That day, I came back from a meeting to find Brendan's body in the study. He had a plastic bag over his head and there were two empty tablet bottles by his side. I barely recognized him. The last time I saw him was that morning in the kitchen, making himself a mug of coffee. He'd left it there on the desk, not drunk. It was a chilling scene. I felt pain, but didn't have any emotions, not even sadness or anger. I phoned for an ambulance as calmly as if I were booking a taxi. At the time, I thought I'd never feel anything again.

The shattering effect of finding the body can alter us irrevocably. Death is rarely a clean and tidy affair and, even more disturbingly, it could have taken place in your car, house or garage. A relative, friend or complete stranger might be the first to walk into the scene of the act. The sight of the body is always an immense shock, especially if it is mutilated, burned or destroyed beyond recognition. The method used may leave blood or vomit, and there may be upsetting signs of chaos or personal struggle.

Naomi describes her feelings at finding her daughter Emily's body early on a Sunday evening. Emily had slashed her wrists.

> It's like an eternal moment in time. It was over five years ago, but

10

I can still see every stark detail. She was slumped on our bathroom floor. The bath was full of water that was red with blood. Her long hair covered her face and her dressing gown was blood-drenched. For just a second I told myself it was someone else, *anyone* else, but not my daughter. I reached to pull her hair back, but I knew it was Emily. Her face was drained and her eyes were staring into nothingness. I screamed until my neighbour came round. Although the images are still vivid, at least they're less painful to me now. When the pictures come flooding into my mind I push them away gently and try to think about the positive aspects of her life.

Regardless of whether you stumble on the body or receive the news through someone else, your immediate reactions are likely to be devastating. You will always remember the moment you found the person, the telephone rang, or there was a knock at your door. It's only human. Before it touched your own life, you might have imagined that suicide was rare. You could also have assumed that a loved one about to take their own life would have revealed clues about their unhappy state of mind, but so often they don't.

For these first terrible hours, you'll understandably be reeling from shock. When it feels as though things can't possibly get any worse, the disaster pitches you into a realm of post-mortems, coroners and undertakers. Strangers intrude at a time when the initial helpless feelings after the death still consume you. Although you need support right now, these people are there to investigate what took place. The cold nature of the procedures and making of statements confronts you with the harsh reality. The words you hear – suicide, self-killing, overdose, asphyxiation, shooting or drowning – all have a new and gruesome meaning for you. It's also the first time you've heard your loved one referred to as 'the deceased' or 'the body'.

The numbness of the initial shock may be a blessing that helps to see you through this bewildering experience. You may endure any number of physical symptoms including headaches, a churning stomach, nausea, sleeplessness or feeling shaky. The surge in your adrenaline at this time can make everything feel surreal. You probably feel as though you want to do something, but you can't. You feel helpless.

11

Stella found her son hanging in his bedroom two days after his seventeenth birthday:

> I was stupefied. All my feelings were frozen and I couldn't even cry. The full impact came when the numbness wore off. My emotions were raw and I became hysterical, shouting at everyone who came near me. I thought I would choke with fear. It was hard to accept that other people go about their usual business and the world seemed oblivious to his death. Our son had just killed himself and our lives could never be the same again. We had crossed the threshold into a completely new universe.

Occasionally, a child is the first person to find the body of a family member. It could be their parent, grandparent, brother or sister. Some may even witness the suicide. It's difficult to imagine the enormity of the impact this can have on their lives and they are likely to need considerable understanding and reassurance from the adults in their life.

Post trauma stress disorder

After any shock or disaster, it's common for us to suffer from extreme stress. Post trauma stress disorder (PTSD) can affect witnesses and survivors of a suicide. The symptoms that might indicate PTSD include:

- Recurring recollection of the suicide.
- Dreaming about the event.
- Feeling the suicide is actually recurring.
- Feeling detached from other people.
- Avoidance of things that remind you of the suicide.
- Having persistent unwelcome thoughts.
- A sense of unreality and feeling helpless or confused.

These symptoms can be very frightening and you may want to seek help from a therapist who specializes in post trauma stress disorder. Everyone has different needs at a time like this, though, and some find that the support they receive from family and friends is enough to get them through it.

Meeting immediate needs

The instant disruption to normal life or family routine can make you feel completely out of control of events. This is a time when the assistance of friends and family is paramount. You may need practical help with children, for instance, or with any responsibilities that you can no longer meet. One of the decisions you have to make is whether you should see the body, and if you do, you'll almost certainly want someone to be with you. You're likely to feel as though you're functioning at a basic survival level at this time and have little energy or motivation. The most important thing is just getting through each day, but try to remember to eat and get some rest even if you don't feel like it.

First denial

The sudden and often violent death of someone you care about leaves you emotionally paralysed. Denial usually steps in to take over, though. Your reaction may be to reject the evidence, in an attempt to hold back the terrible pain in the immediate aftermath of the death. You're unable to accept that your loved one ended their life in suicide, despite the compelling signs to suggest that they did. This sense of disbelief may be the only mechanism you have for dealing with the distressing facts. You might hear the details repeated several times, but are unable to take them on board. This is a perfectly normal reaction for we often come to terms with terrible news by piecing together what happened and accepting the truth bit by bit.

Inevitably, you will experience powerful swings of emotion, which may range from sorrow to rage to disbelief. Ken's daughter was 28 when she jumped from a bridge while on a working holiday in California:

In the first few days, you hope there's been a terrible mistake and it's not a suicide after all. My imagination knew no bounds in coming up with an alternative explanation. I refused to accept that Donna had committed suicide. Something else *must* have happened. A gang of thugs pushed her, or someone made her jump. Perhaps it was a tragic accident. She was walking on the parapet of the bridge for a dare and then she fell. When I realized that my wife seemed sceptical about my ravings, I was convinced I was going mad. I felt she was giving up too easily by accepting the simplest conclusion. I couldn't bear to imagine that our daughter thought so little of herself to jump to her death. The facts of her death seeped into my consciousness gradually and it was some weeks before I finally accepted what was staring me in the face. Donna had been desperately unhappy and took her own life.

A cruel rejection?

We could perceive suicide as the ultimate rejection of society and its values, or even a rebuff to life itself. Although it's possible you will see it as an act of defiance against the universe, it's much more likely you'll feel it's a final and cruel rejection of you.

Jake's wife Wendy took a lethal dose of painkillers and tranquillizers. She was a personal assistant to a solicitor and had always been ambitious. The couple faced a major setback when the price of their London flat fell dramatically, leaving them in negative equity. Wendy had worried constantly that they were trapped and unable to move. Jake said, 'It really got to her, you know. I thought that as we were in trouble together, that we would solve it together. I can't believe she did this without telling me. I feel utterly hurt and betrayed.'

You may feel as though your loved one turned their back on you or punished you. What makes it harder is that everyone can see that the individual has seemingly abandoned you. You might feel very bitter in the early stages, but your perception of their motives for suicide are likely to change as you begin to recover.

Dispelling the myths

Society frequently deals with suicide in hushed voices and there are countless myths surrounding it. We might all be more knowledge-able about the subject if it were more openly debated. If any aspects of these misconceptions apply in your situation, you have no reason to feel bad about it. In the circumstances, it's not surprising that you didn't know the facts beforehand. Some of the myths are:

People who talk about suicide never do it

This is certainly not true, and it's potentially a highly dangerous misconception. A significant percentage of victims do discuss, or at least mention, the possibility of suicide to someone else. The Samaritans, for example, lend an ear to many people who desperately want to talk about killing themselves before taking any action.

You can't stop a determined person from killing themselves

Although this assumption may be true for a few individuals, it isn't always the case. Sometimes people reach the extreme decision to take their own life because they can't think of an alternative escape from their misery. At least we can help just by listening, talking, and offering concern and sympathy. There is always a chance that we may get the person to consider other possibilities or see there is hope for them. Of course it doesn't always work, but it is possible to initiate a change in a person's intention.

Suicide is just an easy way out

This view comes from the perception that the individual has a weak character and, as a result, they fail to cope with the trials and disappointments in life. Some people might say, 'Well, I dealt with a divorce, so why couldn't he?' Although many of us have similar life experiences, they affect each one of us differently. The reality is that all kinds of people, including those who appear to be strong, are vulnerable to taking their own lives.

Anyone with serious intentions leaves a suicide note

The fact that only a small proportion of individuals leave a suicide note or letter of explanation may come as a surprise. Of course, if there isn't a note it can sometimes be difficult to establish whether it was a suicide or an accident.

If someone is in crisis, don't mention suicide

There is usually no real concern about raising the topic of suicide with someone who is depressed or in crisis. Anyone who feels desperate enough will probably already have considered suicide as an option. Having the opportunity to share their anxieties with someone else may encourage them to seek a more positive solution to their despair.

Telling family and friends

It's always hard to tell other people about a suicide as you don't know what their response is going to be. You must expect them to be as stunned as you were. If you work out what to say beforehand, then it'll be easier to find the right words. Try not to confuse people by using euphemisms for death, such as 'We've lost him'. It's better to be clear and say, 'Keith died'. It's perfectly all right to let others make some calls for you. The police, the doctor or other family members are usually willing to help. Your entire existence has been shattered, and no one expects you to be able to function as normal.

When Claire's 71-year-old husband killed himself through carbon monoxide poisoning in their garage, she found the thought of facing up to people's reactions excruciating. 'I just couldn't say the word "suicide". I told everyone, including our daughter, that he'd met with a dreadful accident. When they asked me what happened, I said that no one knew.' It was some days before Claire felt able to tell her daughter and friends the truth.

Parents normally take on the task of breaking the news to their children. In most cases, it's bound to come as a total shock. Often children weren't aware of any pre-existing problem. They might not have known, for example, that their mum, dad or other family member was ill, depressed or alcohol-dependent. From their point of view, the death comes entirely unexpectedly. Some children ask few questions and are satisfied with simple explanations. Others may be more curious and ask continual questions. It's usually best to deal with these as they arise. It's important to be clear that the person has died, rather than has 'gone away' or is 'sleeping', otherwise the child might not grasp that the loss is final. Young children may find the news hard to take in, and so it's often necessary to repeat some of the information. You may have to start by explaining what suicide is, taking into account the child's age and level of development. You can tell them that some people die from accidents, old age or cancer, and that a small number take their own lives.

Joe was seven when his dad fell asleep at the wheel of his car, resulting in a serious road accident in which a woman was badly injured. Two days before the court case his dad poured petrol over his clothes and set himself on fire. It was a horrific way to die and although Joe's mother was still in shock, she explained the reasons for the suicide in a way he could understand: 'Daddy's car crash made him feel so terrible that he couldn't face going on with life. We're all sad that he died, but he wants us to go on living and be happy.' After the funeral she also talked with Joe about better ways in which people could try to solve their problems.

Stick to the facts as far as you can, but avoid any upsetting details that aren't necessary for children's understanding. Honesty is important; half-truths and lies will inevitably be uncovered and be counterproductive. Children are usually very alert in picking up worrying snippets of information from adults. They probably already know that a terrible, unspeakable thing has happened. But what children might conjure up in their imaginations is potentially far more frightening than the truth. It is better to resist the temptation to pass on your own moral viewpoint, such as whether you think the suicide was right or wrong, as children will work this out for themselves as they get older. Using a straightforward approach to telling children avoids anxiety and confusion.

Summary

- Witnesses to the suicide, the person who finds the body, family and friends are all likely to suffer from shock.
- Those who are left behind after the death of a loved one often need immediate help in terms of both practical and emotional support.
- Denial is a normal response to the death of a loved one and it can take weeks or months for the facts of the suicide to sink in.
- Some of the myths surrounding suicide can lead to misunderstandings, so factual information is important.
- Finding the right words to tell other people about the suicide is always difficult, but it's usually best to be straightforward.

3
Suicidal Risk

Almost anyone could find themselves in a position where they would consider suicide, but is there any way of telling who is most susceptible? There appear to be a number of risk factors; however the presence of one or more of these does not mean a person will necessarily take their own life. Only a comparatively small number of individuals will choose death as a way of dealing with, or escaping from, their problems.

The role of stress

One of the main indicators for suicide is a high level of stress. We seem to lead increasingly demanding lives, and the stresses related to work, home or family all play a part in our state of well-being. Stress is a basic response to any threatening situation, regardless of whether the danger is real or imagined. Its function is to prepare our physical strength and mental alertness in order to either fight or run away from immediate danger. Stress arises even if we're not at imminent risk, and everyday activities such as driving and shopping frequently induce high levels in some people. It isn't our experiences, but instead the meaning we give to them, that determines our response to stress. Two people in similar circumstances will respond in quite different ways, so what causes stress for one may not affect the other. We can't avoid stress altogether, and we need a certain amount of it in order to function at an optimum level. When it becomes too much, though, it can engulf us and put our physical and emotional health at risk.

Employment

Certain occupational groups are at increased risk of suicide. These include medical personnel such as doctors, dentists, anaesthetists, nurses, vets and pharmacists. The main reasons for this increased risk appear to be the high levels of stress suffered by people in such jobs and the fact that they have access to the potential means of

18

suicide through drugs and poisoning. Farmers and agricultural workers are also vulnerable. They often have to cope with stress and isolation and their occupation gives them access to firearms. Other high-risk groups include forestry workers, students and teachers in higher education.

Bullying at work

Large organizations, including Ford and the Metropolitan Police, are trying to tackle problems of bullying and institutional racism, which can have a devastating effect on some employees and reduce workforce morale. An individual who has to tolerate bullying, harassment or abuse at work may suffer from depression, sickness, anxiety and stress, so it's a risk factor in adult suicide.

Unemployment

Although being out of work isn't a direct cause of suicide, it often leads to other problems that increase the risk. These include homelessness and housing problems, debt, relationship difficulties and offending behaviour. The inability to find or retain a job or to secure a regular income can put individuals under immense pressure. It also has the potential to undermine their confidence and self-esteem.

Age

One age-related group vulnerable to suicide is young people in their teens and early twenties. Young males in particular are at increased risk, although young females make more suicide attempts. Suicide rates level out for 30- to 40-year-olds and then climb with increased age. When people reach 55, they are at a higher risk of taking their life, and this becomes even more apparent in the 75-plus age group. A disproportionate number of older people suffer from chronic illness and may decide their quality of life is so poor that they would rather die in peace than continue suffering. Also, when a spouse or partner dies in later life, the survivor may not be able to face the future alone. Losses that may add to their burden include retirement, loneliness or depression, one or more of which could increase their susceptibility to suicide.

Race

An individual's race and cultural background will influence their vulnerability to suicide. Countries vary widely in the pattern of suicide in each of their ethnic populations. In the United Kingdom, one report indicated that young Asian women have a suicide rate three times that of British white women in the same age group. This difference may arise because of the conflict between traditional family values, especially in respect of arranged marriages, and Western society's more liberal attitude to relationships. Unfortunately, we know little about the rates and trends of suicide among black men and women in the United Kingom, as there is a lack of related data on race and ethnicity.

Gender

Men are three times more likely than women to kill themselves. It's impossible to single out a particular reason for this difference, and so it's likely to result from a combination of factors. Men are sometimes more reluctant than women to talk about their feelings, and are less likely to visit their doctor with either physical or mental health concerns. In the United Kingdom, boys are currently doing less well at school than girls, and they have a higher chance of being unemployed when they leave. Further pressures have arisen in recent years through the breakdown of traditional gender roles. The concept of the 'new man' has cast many into a sea of uncertainty about what society, women, and other men expect of them. As we have seen, females are far more likely than males to make a suicide attempt, but only a small percentage of these attempts are fatal. The motivation for female attempts is often related to problems or crises in personal relationships. Another important factor in the fatality rate is that men and women also differ in the methods they use. The less successful method of drug overdose commonly used by females almost certainly influences their low rate of completed suicides.

Social isolation

Some people live alone by choice, while others have had it imposed on them through death, separation or through friends and family moving away. Individuals who are lonely and have little social contact, or no close relationships with others, are inclined to be at risk. In particular, men who are not married or in a stable relationship tend to have higher rates of depression and suicide.

Family history

A family history of completed suicide appears to increase the risk of suicide. Researchers are unable to agree about the existence of a genetic tendency to self-harm and, in any case, suicide is an individual act and the reasons for each one are almost certainly multi-layered. The family influence may well arise from associated circumstances. Depression, other mental illnesses, alcohol and drug problems, for example, can affect more than one family member. A bereavement in the family, regardless of the cause, is also a factor for subsequent depression in surviving relatives.

Some of us with a family history of suicide believe that we might one day feel compelled to take our own lives. Although I've always regarded my mum's decision as a rational one, a sense of destiny lingers on and I worry that I may end my life in the same way. I often have to remind myself that my mum's situation was unique and that whatever the future brings, my personal circumstances and my response to them will be different.

Mental illness

Mental disorders, especially depression and schizophrenia, are frequently associated with suicide. The reasons are undoubtedly complex, although the risk seems to be greatest when a personal or family crisis affects the individual. Patients recently discharged from psychiatric hospital are at an increased risk of self-harm and suicide. This is generally presumed to follow a deterioration in their mental health once they leave a highly supportive environment.

Seasonal affective disorder (SAD) is a pattern of recurrent episodes of depression, which emerge during certain months of the year. The most common form is 'winter depression' in which individuals are affected by low moods during the winter months when there is less daylight around. SAD usually results in mild to moderate depression, but the low moods can be severe and increase the risk of self-harm and suicide.

Substance misuse

The short- and long-term effects of excessive alcohol or drug use can contribute to attempted or completed suicide. Substance misuse is a way of covering up emotions that are too difficult to deal with. People frequently use alcohol to relieve stress, anxiety and depression, without realizing that it acts as a powerful depressant drug. Although initially it may help them to blot out feelings of despair, ultimately the alcohol will enhance their symptoms. The physical and psychological effects of dependence on opiates such as heroin, stimulants, tranquillizers and other drugs can lure people into a downward spiral, with all aspects of their lives being affected.

Physical illness

Patients suffering from chronic or terminal illness are extremely susceptible to suicide. Many conditions are painful and debilitating, even if they aren't immediately life-threatening. Motor neurone disease, multiple sclerosis, spinal cord injuries, chronic fatigue syndrome and aggressive cancers understandably lead people to feel hopeless about the future. Some medications that cause symptoms of depression, such as steroids and anti-cancer drugs, may put a patient at greater risk of suicide. Although illness and pain principally affect older people, a number of chronic conditions can also make young people's lives unbearable. Examples of those illnesses that are known to increase the risk of suicide include diabetes mellitus, HIV/AIDS and Huntington's chorea.

After crisis or loss

Any crisis or bereavement can lead an individual to feel anxious, bewildered or depressed. A loss could occur through an abortion, redundancy, divorce or a financial disaster, as well as through the death of someone close. It's crucial to be aware that if you are coping with the loss of a loved one, the stress this creates may make you vulnerable to suicide. If you experience persistent suicidal thoughts, there is a good chance that this is a symptom of depression, and therefore an illness rather than a normal response. In this eventuality, you would need to seek the advice of your doctor.

Homelessness

Homeless people are at an increased risk of suicide. Individuals living on the streets are the 'visibly homeless', but they only represent a small proportion of people who are unable to secure a home. Many are staying in emergency hostels or in other temporary or insecure accommodation. Homelessness is associated with other significant factors including unemployment and mental illness. Some homeless people lead chaotic and dangerous lifestyles through alcohol and drug dependence, and may be trapped in a destructive cycle that can lead to them ending their lives in suicide.

Imprisonment

In most countries, the suicide rate for prisoners is much higher than it is for the general population. Young men held in prisons and young offender institutions are particularly vulnerable. In the United Kingdom, self-inflicted deaths of prisoners have doubled over the past ten years. The majority of these suicides occur in the initial three months of detainment. Prison staff routinely put prisoners who are assessed as high risk on 'suicide watch' during this time. The prison service operates a 'listener scheme' in which the Samaritans organization trains prisoners to offer help and support to fellow inmates who are being bullied or feel anxious, depressed or suicidal.

Gay and lesbian identity

There is some evidence from both the United Kingdom and the United States to suggest that gay men and lesbians are at increased risk of suicide and attempted suicide. Families, friends and society can lack tolerance of individuals who they regard as non-conforming. In addition, the legislation related to housing, employment, pension and insurance rights is often restrictive for these groups. Personal experiences of rejection or discrimination can lead to a lack of self-esteem and confidence.

Access to means

If the methods for carrying out a suicide are readily available to an individual with suicidal thoughts, the risk increases. People who've decided to kill themselves are inclined to use whatever methods readily present themselves. A wide range of medical staff routinely have access to lethal drugs. In the United States, people commonly use guns, as they are widely available. Local areas and communities in most countries have their own bridges and buildings that become associated with suicides. As mentioned earlier, there are certain groups of people in the United Kingdom that are likely to own firearms. In the early stages of the foot and mouth crisis of 2001, many farmers throughout the country watched their livestock – and, in some cases, their whole livelihoods – burn on funeral pyres. Local police encouraged the badly affected – and very often depressed – farmers to hand in their shotguns to minimize the chances of them being used by the farmers as a means of taking their own lives.

Previous suicide attempts

A history of self-harm is a significant risk factor, especially if the attempts were medically serious. Self-harming behaviour often runs deeper than our common perception of it as just attention-seeking, and it may indicate a high level of stress or despair. When an individual makes repeated suicide bids it's easy to think the risk isn't serious. The likelihood of an attempt ending in death, however, increases with the number of attempts made.

Murder-suicide

It is well documented, but extremely rare, that an individual committing a murder may kill themselves shortly afterwards. This may result from a personality disorder, or the individual's intense frustration and inability to cope with a life that has become intolerable for them. Multiple killers who go on the rampage also run a high risk of turning the weapon against themselves. They might be motivated to kill themselves through feelings of defeat or misery, or to avoid facing the consequences of arrest and trial.

Risk and prevention

As certain factors expose people to suicide, we may assume it's feasible to determine the risk and then prevent the tragedy from occurring. Medical and social work professionals use a number of measures to assess people in their care who might be in danger of self-harm. While there is undoubtedly value in monitoring those believed to be vulnerable, this is immensely difficult in practice. The unique combination of individual circumstances, history, and mental and physical illness makes it hard to evaluate the suicide risk.

Living with a suicidal person

Sharing your everyday life with someone you care about who wants to die can be terrifying. You're afraid they'll kill themselves while you're asleep, at work, or out doing the shopping. You worry that a harsh word or a misjudged action will push them over the edge and trigger suicide. The individual may be depressed or have made one or more previous attempts. Sometimes it's impossible to know whether it's best to hold out a helping hand to the person or to stand back and let them work things out for themselves. You probably feel as though you're balancing on a knife-edge. Sadly, you're an audience to your loved one's personal nightmare and are powerless to rescue them. When you're close to the individual, you find their pessimism and low self-worth hard to understand. If they seem to have lost all hope in their life, you may feel desperate to find solutions for them. To be honest, there's probably little you can do. Meaningful change only begins when the person can see there is a future for them.

There are many people in a similar position to you and, without exception, they find it overwhelmingly difficult. The anxiety is inevitable and it doesn't mean you're doing anything wrong. Whatever happens, you're not to blame for the individual's depression any more than you would be if they had cancer or heart disease. Although you'll inevitably do whatever is in your power to help, it's crucial to be aware of the limitations of your responsibility. Friends and family can offer love, encouragement and support, but your loved one's state of mind may not allow them to recognize it or accept it. They can feel demoralized, inadequate and hopeless. It's also common for the people you care about to conceal their suffering from you and others who want to help them. All you can offer is a continual reminder to your loved one that they have options other than suicide.

You are living in a stressful situation and are therefore vulnerable to exhaustion, physical illness and depression yourself. When events overstretch your resources, it's difficult to remain optimistic and offer hope to a loved one in crisis. If you're living with someone who is depressed and at risk of self-harm it's essential to take care of your own physical and emotional health.

Summary

- A number of factors including stress, occupation, health and gender, affect suicide rates and patterns.
- People who kill themselves may have a perceived reduction in their reasons for living. This could be because of illness, alcohol and drug use, loss, isolation or other social factors.
- Individual circumstances and the way a person reacts to them can increase stress and make them more susceptible to suicide and attempted suicide. Only a small number of people in high-risk groups will actually take their lives.
- Living with someone who is feeling suicidal, or has already made a suicide attempt, is extremely demanding, so looking after your own needs is vital.

4
Youth Suicide

It's always tragic when a young person dies. If the fatality is self-inflicted, it can be even more shocking. The death has a devastating effect on the individual's family, friends and the community. Youth suicide is a highly charged issue, and in the past the parents took on much of the blame and guilt for the death of their child. Although we've come a long way in acknowledging influences outside of the family circle, sometimes we find it hard to accept that children and young adults experience genuine suicidal feelings. Consequently, we struggle to explain why young people should choose to die.

Young people at risk

Although it's extremely rare for children under 12 to take their own lives, the rate increases significantly after the onset of puberty. In the United Kingdom the suicide rate in the 15–25-year age group has risen by 85 per cent since the 1960s. The incidence in youth is approximately three male suicides to every one female suicide; however, the rates vary in different countries.

For many young people the journey from childhood to adulthood is a challenging undertaking. It is certainly an intense phase of development, with rapid changes occurring both physically and emotionally. Adolescents deal with the upheaval and conflict in different ways. Parents may say they felt they had little understanding of the issues that were dominant in their children's lives at this crucial time. These young people might have felt angry, lonely, a failure, sensitive to criticism, or ashamed in a way that appeared out of proportion to their problems.

Attempted youth suicide and self-harm

Attempted suicide has reached epidemic proportions and there are 19,000 reported suicide attempts by adolescents in the United Kingdom every year. Self-harm behaviours vary in the extent to which they are life-threatening and the individual's desire to die may be ambivalent. The rate for both males and females increased during the 1990s, with females between the ages of 15 and 19 being most likely to make a suicide bid. An act of self-harm is sometimes used to:

- Gain relief from physical or emotional pain.
- Try to be understood, or taken seriously.
- Frighten someone.
- Make someone feel sorry for you.
- Persuade someone to change their mind.
- Make someone care about you.
- Find out if a particular person loves you.
- Show how much you love someone.

Some adolescents find it difficult to communicate their troubles to their parents and other adults and to have their feelings recognized. Amy was 15 when a build-up of events threatened to overwhelm her:

> Everything crashed in on me when my boyfriend said it was over. I was gutted. At home, I got into a bitter argument with my sister over a jacket she'd borrowed and ruined. My mum said 'it was for the best' that Tim and I were finished. How could she say that? I thought the whole world hated me. I got my dad's sleeping tablets from the bathroom cabinet and shut myself in my room. I shook the bottle of pills out on to my bed. I couldn't think of anything good about my life, it just felt unbearable. I only wanted to stop the pain. I took 12 pills with a can of coke. The next thing I remember was waking up in the hospital. I was so relieved to see my mum there at my bedside.

Risk factors in youth

Although children and young adults are subject to similar risk factors as adults, several of these are particularly influential.

Depression and young people

The diagnosis of depression in adolescents has risen over recent years. This invites speculation as to whether young people are finding life increasingly difficult to cope with or, alternatively, simply that the medical profession is getting better at identifying the illness. Depression in adolescence tends to be associated with a reaction to particular life events. However, those most likely to experience depression are individuals whose mother or father, or both, are prone to depression themselves. In experiencing a low mood for the first time, teenagers and young adults often fail to recognize it as a transitory state. Suicide is often said to be a long-term solution to a short-term problem.

Alcohol and other drugs

Many young people who find it difficult to cope with their problems seek an escape through drink or drugs. Others use them for recreation and they can become an integral dimension of their social activities. One example is young people taking the drug ecstasy to heighten their enjoyment of dance and other events. Over time, youngsters may become dependent on one or more substances. It's a popular misconception that illegal drugs carry greater risks than alcohol for the young, and the media seem keen to highlight accidental and suicidal deaths in which cocaine, ecstasy or heroin has played a role. While every incident involving drugs is certainly tragic, the reality is that in the United Kingdom drinking takes a much heavier toll on our youngsters' lives. When young people aren't used to alcohol, it affects them very quickly. Consequently, they are susceptible to accidents, violence and risk-taking activities. Young women appear to be drinking more than they used to and their consumption is catching up with that of young men. Disturbingly, each year around one thousand young people under 15 are admitted for emergency treatment for alcohol poisoning.

If you are a parent, you might get embroiled in a battle to rescue your son or daughter from misuse of alcohol and other drugs. As the father of one 19-year-old explained:

We tried to get Steve to cut down on his nightly drinking binges. He couldn't hold down a job because he'd never get up before two o'clock in the afternoon. We were concerned about what sort of future he would have. At one point we were so desperate, we bribed him to go to a counsellor. He didn't keep all of his appointments and he became morose and impossible to live with. We worried that the booze would kill him if he did something stupid under the influence. He lost his ability to reason things out and was continually involved in fights after heavy drinking bouts. We thought it could only get better, but it just got worse. He always went out with friends who drank and we had no power to put the brakes on his self-destructive course. Last February he became mindlessly drunk, fell into a canal and drowned. Now he's dead we realize we actually lost him a very long time ago. We've suffered over the years and I think we'd already grieved over the son that wasn't to be.

Twenty-first century demands

The ever-increasing pressures of contemporary life tend to be blamed for the high suicide and attempted suicide rate in young people.

Self-image

The popular media assail us with images of attractive, and sometimes painfully thin, role models. This may influence the expectations of young people struggling with their emerging identity and self-image. Until recently, eating disorders were predominantly associated with women, but anorexia nervosa and bulimia are now becoming more prevalent among young men. Eating disorders are frequently associated with depression and low self-esteem, and so increase the risk of self-harm and suicide.

If an individual feels dissatisfied with their weight, the shape of their nose, or the colour of their hair, they may be in danger of becoming obsessed with what they *perceive* as a serious and intolerable defect. They imagine or exaggerate the flaws they see in themselves. The individuals may well be attractive, yet other people telling them they look good or beautiful doesn't make them feel any better about themselves. This condition, known as 'body dimorphic disorder', doesn't just affect young people, and it crosses gender boundaries. In many cases the person recognizes it's a psychological rather than a physical condition, but this insight doesn't prevent them from feeling the way they do.

30

Lauren is a dental nurse who lives with her boyfriend:

I think about my face all the time. It looks hideous and I can't understand how other people can look at me without being revolted. Last year I had my nose reshaped but it only made a slight improvement. I wear make-up to conceal my features but it's not enough to make me feel confident or accept my appearance. I compulsively check myself in the mirror, hoping I don't look as bad as last time I looked, so I get increasingly obsessed. People think I'm vain, but deep down I feel ugly and useless. I've attempted suicide several times, usually when the stress and embarrassment about my problem gets too much.

Some children have physical deformities from birth or suffer through illness or disease. Acne, psoriasis and atypical facial features can be excruciating to live with if you are young, and those affected are sometimes bullied because they look different.
Insensitive remarks can destroy self-esteem:

Carl is 19 and has a severe skin disorder that makes his life a misery. 'I have terrible flare-ups of psoriasis and I can't accept how terrible I look. A woman at the supermarket told me I was a "disgrace" and that I should keep away from her children. I felt crushed and despondent. In the end, the stress became intolerable and I took an overdose of paracetamol.' As a result Carl suffered liver damage, but is now recovering and has started treatment for his depression.

Expectations

We live in an achievement oriented society in which expectations of academic work and career success are growing. Some young people just sail through their exams. Others, though, find the stress and anxiety daunting and feel unable to cope with the demands. In 1999, two teenagers in Buckinghamshire hanged themselves within six days of each other before they were due to sit important examinations. The coroners' verdict in both cases was that a combination of pressures, including exams, had contributed to the deaths.

Alvin attempted to kill himself after he learned he'd failed to make the A-level grades he needed. Luckily, his father discovered him in time to call the emergency services. Alvin is the youngest of three children. His elder brothers had left school at 16 and Alvin carried his parents' hope that he would become a vet like his dad. He saw his failure to achieve the necessary exam grades as letting down his parents. 'I knew my performance would disappoint my family as they expected me to get grade As. At the last minute I panicked and couldn't face telling them.'

Some youngsters do succeed in killing themselves when they are shocked or disappointed at their exam grades. Others are so convinced they've failed that they don't even wait for the results to come out.

At one time, it was usual for people to work for many years to reach the top of their employment or profession. These days, however, there is increasing pressure on young people to be successful early on in their careers. Some do achieve this, particularly in the field of information technology and Internet businesses where high achievers are often in their twenties and early thirties. This is also linked with expectations of earning a salary that will support a good standard of living, which may include financing a car or property, clothes, travel and leisure activities. If young people don't achieve their goals quickly, then they may feel that they've failed.

Relationships

Young people have a need to establish new relationships as they progress through school or college. Difficulties often arise in their sexual relationships, or there might be conflict with their parents or people in authority. Adolescence is a critical time for developing your sexual identity, and some may be uncertain of their sexuality. They may feel that family and friends don't understand them and are anxious about discussing it in case they are faced with disapproval or discrimination.

Problems with the law

Young people often get into trouble with the police, particularly through offences of theft, criminal damage and car-related crime. A build-up of pressures in coping with the police, the courts and sentences may lead to high stress levels and depression, with the associated risk of suicidal behaviour.

Family influence

A disruptive family life affects some youngsters deeply and makes them more likely to self-harm. Death, divorce or trauma in a family can lead to a breakdown of relationships and an unsettled existence for the children. If the parents are unemployed or suffer from mental illness or substance dependence, the evidence suggests that their children are at increased risk of suicide. Do remember, though, that many youngsters who attempt suicide have enjoyed a happy and settled childhood, so no family is immune from the tragedy. Indeed, it's common for there to be conflict in any household during the teenage years, and family rifts may lead to suicide in the most caring and supportive families. If you experienced problems with your son or daughter, it's essential to bear in mind that many of the pressures on the young person were undoubtedly beyond your influence.

Romantic idealism

High-profile suicides always grab the headlines and the public imagination. Reports often idealize the deaths as romantic tragedies, especially when the victims are poets, artists or musicians. The depiction of suicide as valiant, passionate or ill-fated can have serious repercussions for some youngsters who may see it as a positive or desirable act.

Contagious suicide

Contagious suicide is the name given to a theory of suicide by example. Often termed copycat or cluster suicide, young people can be motivated to imitate the self-destructive acts of celebrities, especially if they are raised to the status of a hero, or if the reports sensationalize the suicide. Media coverage that offers a one-dimensional view of the reasons underlying the suicide can mislead people into believing there's a simple explanation and that suicide is a valid response to unhappiness. In Japan in 1986, the teenage idol Yukiko Okada leapt from the seventh floor of her recording studio soon after she'd won an award as Japan's best new singer. Her fans constructed a shrine at the spot where her body landed and there was intense media interest. In the following two weeks, 33 young people killed themselves in Japan, 21 of them jumping from buildings. Although the links are apparent in each of these cases, it may be that the youngsters would have taken their own lives anyway, but using alternative means. Fortunately, the contagious suicide effect tends to be short-lived.

Bullying

Every year a small number of children in the United Kingdom kill themselves following incidents of bullying at school. Many more children make suicide attempts. Types of bullying include calling people names, ignoring them, stealing their possessions or physically attacking them. Sometimes bullies pick on children because of their colour, religion or lifestyle. Racially motivated bullying is prevalent and is increasingly a major cause for concern. Most bullying incidents occur when either the child hasn't felt brave enough to tell anyone, or they did tell someone, but the authorities failed to tackle the abuse. Bullied children are generally younger and smaller than their bullies are, and the evidence suggests that they rarely do anything to instigate the attacks.

In the United States a 14-year-old girl hanged herself after a series of threatening encounters with other girls. She was terrified that her tormentors would kill her if she reported them to the authorities. A 15-year-old girl in Merseyside took her own life after receiving endless anonymous calls on her mobile phone. Threats and bullying via mobile phones, text messaging and e-mail are already increasing in line with the widespread use of these technologies.

Deaths in custody

In the overall prison population, young males are at the highest risk of ending their lives in suicide. This is particularly true of the under-21 age group, who constitute about one-third of those on remand who are awaiting trial. Many young people who end up in prison were severely disadvantaged before their arrest. They may have been unemployed, homeless, abused, or suffered from mental illness or drug or alcohol dependence. Imprisonment frequently increases stress and anxiety, particularly in vulnerable individuals. Fear of the outcome of the trial or the thought of facing a long prison sentence undoubtedly adds to their sense of hopelessness.

Abuse and young people

Traumatic childhood experiences are almost always damaging. Youngsters who have suffered physical or emotional abuse, sexual abuse or neglect are predisposed to develop subsequent mental health problems. They commonly have low self-esteem and are more susceptible to depression, self-harm and suicide.

Warning signs in youth

So how do you know when a young person is thinking about self-harm or suicide? Some of the indications might include:

- Depression, sadness or anxiety.
- Relationship problems.
- Sexual identity crisis.
- Withdrawn behaviour.
- Preoccupation with death and dying.
- Taking unnecessary risks.
- Increased alcohol or drug use.
- Disruptive or violent behaviour.
- Truancy or decline in school work.
- Lack of interest in activities.

It's important to keep in mind that these signs can be extremely difficult to identify, particularly in view of the fact that many could be perceived as normal behaviours in some teenagers.

A young person is likely to be more vulnerable to suicide if they've recently experienced the suicide or attempted suicide of a friend or relative. They may see the act as a way of solving problems, so it can appear to be a viable option when they're having a difficult time. Many young people do seek help in the weeks or months before they kill themselves. They may approach a friend, teacher or a telephone helpline such as Childline or the Samaritans. As a relative, you may be bewildered to find that your loved one shared his or her thoughts with someone else. Although young people occasionally confide in family members, they tend to conceal their real feelings from those they're close to, choosing instead to discuss them with friends, colleagues or even strangers.

Summary

- Suicide and attempted suicide in young people has been increasing over recent years. Young men are at far greater risk of completed suicide than young women.
- For every suicide there are many attempts that are non-fatal, the majority of which are carried out by females. Attempts can be much more than a cry for attention, and an individual making a suicide bid may be deeply confused, disturbed or depressed.
- Youngsters who have a history of suicide attempts are at greater risk of making a further bid, which might be fatal.
- Factors that influence the suicide rate are the pressures of contemporary living, alcohol and drug use, imprisonment and depression.
- The causes of suicide are complex and unique to the individual, although a build-up of stress and anxiety is common.

5

Seeking Understanding

A suicide is rarely straightforward to come to terms with and unanswered questions often haunt those of us left behind. We may feel scared and bewildered by what's happened. It's possible that you'll never know the full circumstances, or what finally moved your loved one to take their own life. Nevertheless, it can help to have an understanding of some of the factors that could have played a part in their fateful decision.

Why did they do it?

The critical question is always 'why?' and it evokes powerful emotions in us. It's hard to give a simple answer because generally suicide isn't a single, isolated act, but the outcome of a long-term process. When looking for answers we tend to focus on stresses in the victim's life that preceded the suicide. Although these recent and more obvious events can be the precipitating factor, they seldom explain the suicide. Realistically, then, we need to consider a number of other aspects of the person's life. These include their past history, family background, and emotional and physical health. The individual's perception and reaction to events, rather than the objective nature of their situation, leads them to suicide.

It isn't unusual for those closest to the individual to be completely unaware of the extent of their loved one's problems. It's possible you had no idea what their thoughts and feelings were in the weeks, days and minutes that led up to their death. So, what might have dominated their thoughts beforehand? Of course, you will never know what was in the mind of your loved one at this critical time, but they may have experienced one or more of the following:

- Wishing that they didn't exist.
- Having an obsession with death.
- Thinking they'd be better off dead.
- Wanting to sleep and not wake up.

37

- Being unable to see any future for themselves.
- Thinking about or planning suicide.
- Having a lack of control over events.
- Feeling worthless and hopeless.

There are many theories about the reasons underlying suicide but, as a survivor, much of this appears irrelevant to your personal dilemma. It's already too late. The person you cared about has died and you just want to make sense of what happened. What did death offer them that made it a more attractive choice than life?

Escaping pain

Suicidal feelings can be a response to acute and unrelenting pain. This may be because of a major event, or a series of disappointments and traumas that build up gradually. If the individual then fails a final exam, becomes ill, or writes off the family car, the stress can be enough to push them over the edge. They may be unable to stop the onslaught of their emotions, and suicide might begin to look like a saviour and a path away from pain.

Alvin, who survived his hanging attempt, explains, 'I convinced myself I was useless and that I couldn't achieve anything. I knew my dad would be disappointed in my exam grades. From my point of view, life was plummeting to unthinkable depths. I didn't want to die. I just wanted to separate myself from the pain. It was the only solution I could think of.' Ending his life seemed to be a way out of the agony for Alvin.

Your loved one may have felt confused, bewildered and defeated. At a time when they were either consumed with emotion, or lacking any feelings, they felt they were ending the *pain* rather than ending their *life*.

Physical illness
People of all ages may consider death as an alternative to suffering from painful and limiting illness. My mum was 38 when she became ill and I think she lost hope gradually, as it became apparent just

how serious her condition was. She realized she had no chance of a cure or recovery and there was no light into the future. I've since drawn strength from her through acknowledging the courage she had in making her decision. Older people with chronic conditions sometimes choose to spare themselves debilitating pain and indignity in their advancing years.

Mental health problems

A range of mental health problems, including depression, distorted thinking or irrational beliefs, may make a person vulnerable to suicide. The most common mood disorders are depression and 'bipolar' disorder, sometimes known as manic depression. The latter is characterized by mood swings of elation and manic episodes, followed by severe depression. Depressive symptoms can range from feeling constantly sad with a lack of any interest in the world, to feeling angry or murderous. Severe depression can be a life-threatening illness in that one common symptom is a wish to die. Suicidal thoughts may constantly spring into the mind for no apparent reason, and the individual can become immersed in them.

You can't always see the reason for your loved one's pain and sadness and this can make it hard to comprehend. The causes of depression are undoubtedly complex, although it's tempting to look for a single explanation. Sometimes it is a reaction to a particular event, but sufferers can't always relate a depressive phase to any external circumstances. On occasion, people take their lives just as they're emerging from a depressive episode. This is an appalling shock as you understandably assumed the worst was over, and that your loved one was getting better. The reason appears to be that while they were in the grip of despair they were unable to act. As the depression lifts, people suddenly have the energy and motivation to follow through the plan.

The high incidence of suicide in people with schizophrenic disorders is often associated with a distortion in their perception and reasoning. They may, however, be in a depressed state at the time they harm themselves.

Excessive use of alcohol and prescription or illegal drugs can lead to physical and mental illness, unemployment, financial problems, homelessness and the breakdown of relationships. The effect of drugs, including crack cocaine and amphetamines, can be to lower restraint, sometimes leading to impulsive suicide attempts. There is a strong association between dependence on these substances and intentional self-harm and suicide.

Loss of hope

Hope is a positive feeling about the future and usually we have an idea in our minds of what we'll be doing tomorrow or next week. Illness, loss and misery can be exhausting and drown our ability to look forward with any sense of optimism. When someone loses sight of the future and has no map to lead the way out of their despair, they may see no reason why they *shouldn't* end their life.

The suicide note

Only around 25 per cent of people who kill themselves leave a note. They may address it to their partner, family, friends, or the world in general. The note can be helpful, or just another confusing piece of the jigsaw you're trying to piece together to reach some understanding. It may also make sense to one person yet completely mystify another, depending on the relationship they had with the deceased person. The purpose of the note may be to:

- Say a final goodbye.
- Make a statement about their physical or mental illness.
- Explain their state of mind and rationale for suicide.
- Blame someone for causing or contributing to their death.
- Blame themselves for their decision.
- Express their dissatisfaction or anger about something.
- Thank the people they love for caring about them.
- Relieve others of the burden of responsibility they might assume, by reassuring them it's not their fault.
- Act as a written will, with directions as to what should happen to children, property or money.
- Provide information or instructions on things they want done.

It's devastating to receive a letter that you can't answer, especially if it's charged with emotion. The sentiments may be bitter, accusatory, kind, loving, sorrowful or apologetic. The message might give you a sickening feeling of guilt, fury or anguish. Alternatively, the written words could be a source of comfort and reassurance, especially if they clarify some of the uncertainty for you. You're likely to come back to it repeatedly in an attempt to interpret the absolute meaning of the words.

After the shock of the suicide there could be a further one in store if the letter reveals new information about your loved one's life. One woman found that her sister had been in a lesbian relationship for more than ten years. She wished she'd known about it beforehand so she could have got to know her sister better, as the person she really was. A young man whose father shot himself discovered that his parents had adopted him as a baby and he felt angry that he had been deceived for so long. Receiving the news can be difficult, and as the police routinely take the note as evidence for the inquest, the contents can sometimes become public before the relatives have been able to read it. Although it may seem highly important now, it can be a good idea to try to keep any written communication in perspective. After all, it's just one part of the mystery. It may be that the individual put pen to paper under extreme stress, and possibly while under the influence of drink or drugs. No matter how clear or passionate the words, the person wrote them at a particular time and in a frame of mind that might not reflect their overall feelings.

Some survivors feel cheated that the individual didn't leave a note. One mother felt extremely bitter that her son hadn't given any clues to the motivations for his suicide: 'He couldn't even be bothered to acknowledge our existence. Now we'll never know why he did it.' She believed a note would have explained everything about the suicide. Although this is a seductive idea, the truth is that suicide notes often confuse and infuriate relatives because they are vague or ambiguous. They don't always answer the questions that are consuming your sanity.

There are occasions when a suicide note is helpful in coming to terms with the loss:

Martin's partner Nick left a detailed suicide letter. Nick wanted to convey how he felt about his life and to reassure Martin that he wasn't responsible for what happened. In writing the letter, he tried to explain his thoughts about what had led up to his depression and the decision to take his life. 'He came to see suicide as a positive way out of his problems. The letter was a journey for him and for me.'

41

Planned and impulsive acts

A suicide that is planned so that no one will be around when it happens is usually a deliberate act. Some people plan their suicide a long time in advance, so they have the opportunity to put their affairs in order before they die:

> Brendan was 24 when his father died of lung cancer. He never really got over losing his dad and had been taking anti-depressants for three years. One Monday afternoon Brendan transferred all the money from his bank and building society accounts into that of his partner, Debbie. The following day he poisoned himself with an overdose of barbiturates. Debbie was stunned when she realized the extent to which Brendan had orchestrated his own death: 'He put some things in my name weeks earlier and his final transaction was to credit all his savings to my account. He'd been quite normal and cheerful in the period leading up to his death and it's hard for me to understand how he could be so rational about it.'

Suicidal acts carried out on impulse can be highly unpredictable. The individual may feel compelled to kill themselves because of a mental illness or through losing their inhibitions or judgement through alcohol or drugs. A suicide that has a chance of success or failure depending on fate could easily be a cry for help, rather than a deliberate attempt to die.

Chosen methods

The method an individual uses to kill themselves could be significant for them and form a part of their planned decision. Alternatively, they may use whatever means present themselves, especially if they are acting on impulse. Consequently, the method chosen doesn't necessarily tell us anything about the motivation for the death.

A formidable catalogue of techniques is used, many of which are disturbing or grotesque to others. The most common methods include poisoning, hanging and the use of firearms. Males tend to use methods that are more active or violent, such as hanging, shooting, carbon monoxide poisoning, or jumping from a height.

These decisive actions limit the chance of rescue. Women are inclined to be more passive in their approach, frequently using drug overdose or drowning. These methods may leave room for others to intervene or for the individual to change their mind. Young Asian women, however, sometimes use the lethal method of setting themselves on fire. The traditional Hindu practice of suttee, where women burn themselves to death on their husband's funeral pyre, may account for this particular choice.

Common methods also include stabbing to the chest or abdomen, and deep cuts to the wrists, arms and legs, which sever major blood vessels. Overdoses of anti-depressants, tranquillizers, sedatives and paracetamol are often combined with alcohol. For those detained in custody, hanging is the usual method adopted, as few other means are available in a prison environment.

There was a significant drop in suicides by gassing when the United Kingdom domestic gas supply changed from coal gas to North Sea gas. The latter is non-toxic, putting an end to the oven and gas fire suicides that were once prevalent. Safety measures on cars and catalytic converters following the alarming rise of suicides by this method have reduced carbon monoxide poisoning deaths. Some individuals using this method can now take more than 24 hours to die.

An overall reduction in the prescribing of barbiturates, and restrictions on tranquillizers such as Valium, has lowered the incidence of deaths through these methods. In 2001, reported deaths from paracetamol and aspirin overdoses in the United Kingdom halved following the introduction of legislation in 1998 to limit the number of tablets in a pack. Despite the evidence that these preventative measures have an impact, it's not clear whether restricting access to these methods reduces the overall suicide rate. It may be that people switch to alternative means when previous ones become unavailable.

When suicide fails

Some people who survive a suicide bid make a full recovery. Unfortunately, though, the attempt can leave others with mild to serious injuries. A significant proportion will suffer permanent

43

health problems or disabilities. A failed hanging, poisoning, jump or drowning can lead to liver damage, coma, brain injury, broken bones or disfigurement. Any attempt that is not completed may result in the victim requiring a high level of support from family, friends and medical services.

A *hostage to hindsight*

There is always regret after a suicide, even if the relationship with the individual wasn't good. It can be appalling to realize that someone close to you intended to take his or her life. You may interrogate yourself relentlessly about the role you played and the things you might have said or done. You've probably run the events leading up to the death over in your mind, agonizing over neglected opportunities and asking yourself how you could have missed the signs. For most people, the behavioural changes that lead up to suicide tend to be gradual. Consequently, it's almost impossible to pinpoint when such a change occurs, thus giving you no warning at all of the potential danger. Some individuals go to great lengths to ensure they don't stir up suspicion and that they won't be disturbed in carrying out the suicide. One young woman told her parents she was staying with friends for the weekend, and let her friends know she was going to spend time with the family. She effectively disappeared and was able to follow through her plan without interference.

When you see, on reflection, a different way you could have responded or helped, you'll understandably wish you'd done something. Anything. But you never know what the outcome would have been had you followed that course. Survivors blame themselves by thinking: 'If only I hadn't owned a gun', 'left the sleeping pills in the cupboard', or 'allowed him to borrow the car'. There's a chance your actions could have averted or delayed the tragedy, but there's no guarantee. The point is that you simply never will know. It's also essential to understand that the suicide was *their* responsibility, not yours. Until you recognize that your loved one alone made the decision to kill themselves, the tyranny of the 'if onlys' of suicide remains.

The warning signs that someone is contemplating taking their life are all too easy to miss even for mental health professionals. They deal with suicide all the time and still they can get it wrong, so it's not surprising that *you* didn't know what was coming. Please don't allow yourself to be a hostage to your thoughts and guilt when you have done nothing wrong.

Surviving without resolution

When you're the person left behind after suicide, you could feel that you owe it to your loved one to understand their motivation. You can devote all your energies to reconstructing their final thoughts and actions in the time leading up to their death. It's persuasive to hope that the individual's last movements might explain why they did it. It's doubtful that you'll be able to determine their rationale, and even if you do, it's not going to change anything. Things can't be undone. No matter how many times you ask yourself why it happened, the death may remain an enigma. It's necessary and helpful to ask questions, but at some point, if they're unanswered, *you need to let them go*. Difficult though it is, for your own sanity you must accept that you may never know why they did it. You have to take a lead in giving yourself the chance to recover and to find future peace of mind and happiness.

Summary

- There are many underlying reasons why people kill themselves. They are usually seeking to escape from their pain, rather than seeking death itself.
- The causes of suicide are multiple and include the interaction of personal circumstances and psychological state.
- Only a minority of people leave a suicide note. The content of a note can either be helpful, or, conversely, confusing and upsetting. Ultimately it may not be possible to wring out a perfect truth about the death from this single source.
- Many different methods are used to commit suicide and their availability to the victim is of prime importance in their choice.
- If someone you care about takes his or her own life, it really isn't your fault. All you can do is your best – and even when friends

45

and relatives do everything possible, it is a fact that some individuals will still kill themselves.

- If there are unanswered questions, at some stage you *must* let them go. You will be making yourself miserable if you continue to pursue answers.

6
Practical Concerns

After a suicide, you may have to deal with a number of practical matters. Attending the inquest, organizing the funeral, and sorting out financial affairs are probably just the first tasks of many. The timing of these demands is always unfortunate, but you do need to address them.

The police investigation

The police investigate the facts and evidence surrounding the death. They interview and take statements from relatives, friends of the victim, witnesses, and the person who discovered the body. The police also gather any physical evidence including the suicide note, drugs found at the scene, or anything that might illuminate the circumstances of the death. You may be clear that your loved one took their own life, but the police must be objective in pursuing their investigation. In certain circumstances, officials may regard you or another family member as a potential suspect in causing the death. This is bound to feel insensitive and exasperating, to say the least. Although it's extremely hurtful to you, it's vital for the police to satisfy themselves that they're dealing with a suicide and not a murder.

The coroner

The police have to inform the coroner of all deaths that are unexpected, violent or accidental. The coroner is usually a lawyer or a doctor who has an independent role in establishing the facts about the death.

The post-mortem

The coroner can order a post-mortem without requiring permission from relatives. Often called an autopsy, this is a detailed examination of the body by a pathologist to verify the actual cause of death.

The pathologist will compile a post-mortem report for the coroner. The coroner then opens an inquest into the death if it was an unnatural or violent death or the cause is not clear.

Attending the inquest

The inquest is a public hearing, so family members and friends are welcome to attend if they wish. You can choose not to go unless the coroner summons you to appear as a witness. The coroner will allow you to suggest calling any witnesses that you think are appropriate. Witnesses read out statements to the court relating to the circumstances of the suicide and the coroner may ask questions to elicit further evidence. The purpose of the inquest is to determine:

- The identity of the deceased.
- How he or she died.
- When the death occurred.
- Where the death occurred.
- By what means the person died.

The procedure in the United States, Canada, Australia and New Zealand is comparable to that of the United Kingdom, although the initial stage may be known as a 'coroner's investigation'. The inquest opens within a few days of the death, after the police have collected all the evidence and the pathologist has submitted the post-mortem. This is usually a brief public hearing which confirms the deceased's identity. It isn't possible to register the death until the coroner has certified the cause. The coroner will normally release the body for burial or cremation and set a date for the full inquest, which may be four to eight weeks later. The delay is even longer in some cases. This is acutely frustrating and you're likely to feel the need to put both the funeral and the inquest behind you before you can move on. The extended wait can keep you in a state of shock and is liable to defer your grieving.

When the law regarded suicide as self-murder and hence a criminal offence, there would have been a trial. The inquest at the coroner's court has now replaced it, although in many ways it retains the character of a trial. Relatives may find the procedure intimidating, and so feel confused or incompetent as they don't know what to expect. It's easy to believe that the court is judging your behaviour, as well as that of your loved one. The coroner, however, isn't concerned with attributing blame or fault for a death, but is simply trying to establish the facts. The inquest is a crucial procedure and you'll probably want to learn as much as possible about how your loved one died. Listening to the witnesses can help you to piece together the evidence and comprehend what happened. Understanding is an important part of the healing process and you need to be satisfied that the court has covered every angle to elicit the truth about the suicide. You *will* get through it. Hearing the witness statements about the death is inevitably distressing, and some of the statements might be hurtful, critical or incorrect. If you prefer not to listen to the more disturbing aspects of the evidence, you can arrange to leave the court temporarily.

The inquest may reveal aspects of the person's life that you didn't previously know about. The individual could have been pregnant, having an affair, ill, or dying of cancer. They might have been living in a gay or lesbian relationship. These new facts can come as a shock, and as they sink in your perception of the suicide might change significantly.

Once the coroner has evaluated all the evidence, he or she will determine the category of death and give a conclusion. The final verdict could be:

- Suicide.
- Natural causes.
- Accidental death or death by misadventure.
- Unlawful killing.
- Open verdict.

When the coroner doesn't think there's enough evidence to support any of the conclusions, he records an open verdict. If further evidence emerges later, it may be necessary to re-open the inquest. In cases where the death could be the result of either an accident or a suicide, the conclusion will normally be accidental death or an open verdict. There are coroners who only reach a suicide verdict in cases where the individual left a note of intention to commit suicide. As only about a quarter of people leave such a note, this suggests that there are considerable gaps in the recording of self-inflicted deaths.

Sometimes a member of the family will destroy the suicide note to conceal the truth about the way their relative died. Also, coroners occasionally bring an open verdict to spare the feelings of relatives, although sadly these deceptions don't help you to come to terms with the loss.

After an inquest, some people admit that they feel disappointed and let down. They hoped it would achieve more than it actually did, by providing a more satisfactory explanation for your loved one's suicide. You may feel it came to a terrible anti-climax and you still have to face your grief and anxieties about the future. It's likely that you will never know any more about your loved one's death than you do now, so it may be time to acknowledge this fact.

An invasion of privacy

The press frequently show up at an inquest and report the findings. The media can treat any death as sensational, but suicide in particular can receive special treatment. If the suicide was violent, linked with drugs, or the person was young, this tends to heighten the news interest. Inaccurate or sensational reporting inevitably causes further misery for family and friends. If the story of your loved one's suicide is exaggerated or mishandled by the press, you may well feel angry and betrayed by their insensitive reporting.

Public exposure is intrusive and, after a self-inflicted death, both the individual who died and the survivors are exposed to society's judgement and, often, society's disapproval. A newspaper article could reveal details of your relationship with the deceased, financial affairs, or mental and physical illnesses that were not public knowledge before the death. Their disclosure unveils the ordeals and suffering of relatives and friends to the outside world. One family was horrified when a newspaper released a photograph of their son's body after he'd jumped from a building.

After such an experience, you'll probably be more alert and sensitive to the portrayal of other suicides in the press. There is little you can do to avoid the discomfort. The family may feel shame at the disclosure of lurid details about the person's life and the manner of death. To you, it's not just a suicide, a story or a statistic, but a person you cared about who had undergone terrible suffering. One way in which you can sometimes pre-empt inaccurate reporting is to contact the newspaper directly with the facts. Do try to remember that the death and the reports written about it are just one aspect of the personal history of your loved one. They do not cast shadows on the entire life of the individual, and the way they lived their life is far more important than the way they died. The news machine moves on and something else will dominate tomorrow's stories.

Arranging the funeral

Organizing the funeral is an emotionally demanding task whatever the cause of death. In the frightening aftermath of suicide, the ritual is an important way of bringing survivors together in their grief.

The ceremony

When there is a death in the family, you need to make some decisions immediately. This is not easy to do, so don't be afraid to call on others in the family to help you think about flowers and choose the music. What sort of funeral would your loved one have wanted? You may have discussed their wishes beforehand, or there may be details in the will. If there are no instructions, the person who is the next of kin normally decides how to proceed. All of us are well advised to leave instructions about the funeral we want, otherwise we're burdening our vulnerable and distressed relatives with making choices on our behalf.

If you are religious, the funeral will be an essential source of comfort for you, whatever your faith. It can create enormous problems when you and your family either have differing beliefs, or none at all. You might feel it's not appropriate to have a religious service if your loved one held no strong convictions. To arrange a non-religious or humanist ceremony, you can contact one of the organizations specializing in these alternative services. It may be worth bearing in mind that it will be impossible to please everyone in the family and, what's more, you don't have to try!

Time spent in planning the event definitely has long-term advantages. The funeral is your opportunity to say goodbye to the person, so you can organize it in a way that has enduring meaning for you. You can choose the music, hymns, flowers and readings to

51

celebrate the highly individual character and interests of your loved one. Usually any speakers at the funeral do acknowledge the fact that the death was a suicide, although naturally the main emphasis should be on the person's life. It may be helpful to consider the opinions of others, but try only to take advice that seems right to you. For instance, you're not obliged to have a church service or prayers if you don't want them.

Adding up the costs

Paying for the funeral is often a worry for those making the arrangements. Traditionally, the family laid out and prepared the body for the funeral. You can still do this and arrange the funeral yourself, although these days most people use the services of a funeral director. Choosing a good one is essential, as they do vary in the level of service they offer and their charges. It helps you to keep within your budget if you get all the information about the costs beforehand. Check that the funeral director is a member of the National Association of Funeral Directors (NAFD) in the United Kingdom or the National Funeral Directors Association (NFDA) in the United States. In other countries, recognized professional organizations have a code of practice for members. A basic 'no frills' funeral will usually include the coffin and hearse. The funeral director pays out fees on your behalf for the cremation, burial and minister's fees, and these are added to your bill. On top of this, you may pay for cars for relatives, flowers, and the funeral gathering. You'll find that burial costs and the price of a plot vary tremendously, but it is usually more expensive than a cremation.

There's no upper limit on what you can spend, but try not to burden yourself with added extras you can't afford. It's easy to be anxious that the amount of money you spend on the funeral makes a statement about how much you loved the person. It doesn't matter. What's more important is that the ceremony itself is a genuine and thoughtful way of saying goodbye. If you are on a tight budget or decide on a simple funeral, it's worth checking with your funeral director how to minimize the expense. The estate of the dead person normally covers the costs and it should be possible to release funds from the deceased's bank or building society account. In practice, the family usually meets the bill and has it refunded from the estate. In cases of hardship, the Social Fund sometimes helps with funeral costs, although the Benefits Agency won't consider a claim if a close family member has the ability to pay. It's feasible that the deceased pre-paid for a funeral while they were still alive; if so, it's worth confirming which items are covered.

Notifying people

There may well be a daunting number of people to inform about the death and the funeral arrangements. The main ones will include the following:

- Relatives and friends.
- Employers and colleagues.
- School, university or college.
- Neighbours and acquaintances.
- Clubs and social circle of the deceased.

Flowers

Those attending the funeral will want to know what to do about flowers. It's possible to send bouquets of flowers, as opposed to wreaths, to a chosen hospital after the funeral. Alternatively, you may want to take the flowers home as a reminder of the funeral. You can request 'no flowers' and invite people to donate the money to a charity, maybe one that was supported by you or your loved one.

Children and the funeral

At one time people thought it was inappropriate for children to attend the funeral. My dad thought my brother and I were too young to be able to cope with Mum's funeral. I know that he was well-intentioned and was hoping to spare us further pain and distress. However, the fact that I never saw her body or took part in this important ritual left me with an enduring sense of unreality about her death. Both my brother and I would like to have been there to share the grief with the rest of our family.

Kiran had a very similar experience:

My dad hanged himself when I was eight and I'm 23 now. I didn't go to the funeral and the family never talked about him. I don't feel as if he's dead. It's odd, but I still imagine that he just left us and went abroad. In my mind, I see him walking around

53

and smiling, with a deep Mediterranean tan. I visit the grave once in a while, but even when I'm there staring at his name on the headstone, it doesn't sink in.

These days it's usual to encourage children to go to the funeral if they want to, although they will need comfort and support. Inevitably they will cry and feel very sad, but it gives them the chance to say goodbye and understand that the person's life is over.

Family reactions

Sometimes a relative won't come to the funeral because they disapprove of the cause of death or they may blame you for it, though they may not be willing to admit this is the reason. Stella's brother and sister-in-law refused to come to her son's funeral: 'The fact that they didn't come felt like a severe punishment to me. I was a mean and uncaring mother and had let him die. I was guilty without trial. I know Adam would have wanted his aunt and uncle to be there.' Everyone affected by a suicide is liable to have heightened emotions in the first few weeks that can affect the judgements they make. Relatives will sometimes behave unfairly to you, although they may very well come to regret this as time goes on.

The funeral gathering

You don't have to invite everyone who attends the funeral to the gathering afterwards, and it's perfectly acceptable to limit it to close relatives and friends. Almost certainly, you won't feel much like meeting people and it's natural to feel dazed and be upset and tearful. Hopefully the people who care about you will join you in your loss and offer you valuable encouragement and comfort.

Rite of passage

Mourning rituals are powerful because they give meaning and structure to our feelings. The funeral is an opportunity to express your sorrow in a socially approved atmosphere. It symbolizes the separation from your loved one and allows you to see you're not alone in your grief. For you, it represents a transition into a new life without the person you cared so much about. It's undoubtedly hard to appreciate the relevance of this now, but it is a new beginning for you.

Stella decided to record her son's funeral ceremony. She knew she would still be in shock and probably wouldn't remember everything that was said on the day. 'It has been a great comfort to play the video back. I'll probably never bring myself to watch it again, but it was important for me to see it.'

Sorting out the loved one's room

You might understandably be tempted to leave the deceased's room untouched for a while. In the short term, you may feel you don't want to disturb any of the personal possessions out of a feeling of respect. Sooner or later, though, you will need to accept the fact that your loved one has died and won't return. Sooner is probably better, and if you leave this task for too long the ordeal of changing their room may be even more daunting. Some parents do keep the room indefinitely as it was, as a shrine to their beloved son or daughter, but this doesn't protect them from the loss. All they're really doing is holding the present at arm's length by trying to freeze the past.

It's always hard to decide what to get rid of and what to hold on to. You could decide to pass items of clothing on to relatives or offer them to a local charity. Of course, it's important to keep photographs, letters and mementoes of your loved one. If there was a suicide note, you might be ambivalent about what to do with it. A letter that contained bitter or hurtful words has the potential to create more distress in the future. There isn't a right answer to this, and it may help to talk it over with other family members.

Dealing with the estate

The executor named in the will is responsible for sorting out the estate. Your loved one may have nominated a bank or solicitor and there is often more than one executor. If they didn't name anyone, or there is no will, then an 'administrator' takes over the deceased's affairs and represents their interests. He or she has the task of settling any debts, taxes or expenses. All payments are made from the estate and then the remainder is shared out in accordance with the will. If the estate is large, you may have to apply for probate to prove the will and to confirm your authority to manage the deceased's finances. Normally it's one of the executors or the main beneficiary who applies. If the person is married, this is normally the spouse. When there's reason to believe there could be liability for inheritance or other tax, the Probate Office should alert you to this.

You can appoint a solicitor to deal with the estate, but do check out their costs first. They may agree a fixed fee, but are more likely to charge you a percentage of the estate, which could turn out to be a considerable sum. Alternatively, you might decide to administer the estate yourself, but it can be a complicated business if many assets are involved. It's very time-consuming, and sometimes distressing, to plough through the personal financial affairs of your loved one. On the other hand, there are advantages in doing it yourself and you will undoubtedly save money. If you need help you can contact a Citizens Advice Bureau, or there are good self-help books available to take you through the steps. Phil acted as executor for his mother's estate: 'It's easy to be put off at the beginning, but actually it was relatively straightforward. I found it satisfying and felt I'd done something on my mum's behalf.'

Living with an inheritance

Your loved one may leave you some of their possessions, family heirlooms or an amount of cash. Heirlooms can be difficult gifts to receive if they're not the kind of things you like to have around you. You might be in debt or need cash urgently, but before rushing to the auction rooms to sell off the inheritance, it may be prudent to find out whether other family members have an interest in them.

It's possible you were expecting to get more than you did, or felt you should have had a particular item. This can create feelings of outrage or jealousy in the family. Try to keep your disappointment or anger in perspective, and remember that your loved one probably didn't intend to upset you.

Inheriting a large sum of money often comes as a terrific shock and is difficult to accept. Many people experience profound guilt over it and one woman said, 'I feel like I swapped my husband for the cash.' Consequently, you may be afraid to spend it, or firmly believe you don't deserve to have it. If you deal with the money thoughtfully, it offers you the chance to make a real difference to your life. You may want to seek the assistance of an independent financial adviser about investments, mortgages or pensions. The deceased left you the money in the hope that you'd enjoy it and have fewer worries, but you don't want to fritter it away. Ideally, you should aim to find a balance between investing some money for the future and allowing yourself to have some benefits now. You won't live for ever, so there's no need to deny yourself too much!

Often, of course, there is no money to inherit. The deceased may have had no financial resources and therefore you need to come to terms with a downturn in your financial circumstances. Whatever the position, you may have to move or sell the house as well as dealing with your unhappiness and grief. If you don't have to make any major decisions straight away, you may be better not doing so. It usually helps to wait until things have settled down. Give yourself time to get over the raw feelings of grief and hopelessness before creating more upheaval and stress for you and your family.

Life insurance

Most life assurance policies decline claims if a death by suicide occurs within the first few years of the policy. Although this is reasonable from the insurer's point of view, it can come as a shock when you had forgotten about the clause, or hadn't fully understood the implications. One of the reasons for a family's reluctance to acknowledge the suicide may be to protect the life insurance claim. Most insurance policies, except those covering death through specific illnesses, will automatically pay out in the case of an accidental death.

Summary

- In addition to your grief, you may have to deal with a number of practical tasks.
- The inquest might seem formal and threatening and your anxiety about it can be overwhelming. Although you may dread attending, many survivors find it a helpful experience.
- Family members frequently express concern and anger about the way in which their loved one's death is reported in the media.

- The funeral is an important occasion for all the relatives and friends, but it's crucial that you arrange it in a way that pleases you.
- Inheriting money and property isn't always easy and you may feel that you don't deserve it. You will have to decide whether to pay a solicitor to deal with the estate, or do it yourself.
- After the death you may find yourself in a worse financial position and could have to move house or make changes to your lifestyle. Unless you have no other option, it's generally wise to defer any major decisions.

7
The Impact of Suicide

The consequences of suicide will affect a large section of the population at some time in their lives. It is often a sudden, unexpected and violent loss. The aftershocks may threaten the foundation of the family and the grief is commonly intense and prolonged. You're probably astounded that such a terrible thing could happen in your own family. It takes a long time for the facts to sink in. Whatever feelings of pain and hopelessness led up to the suicide, your loved one's ordeal is at an end. For you the nightmare is just taking shape.

The surviving family

The family group tends to have a reaction to the death that is distinct from the responses of individuals within it. As each relative had a special relationship with the individual it isn't surprising that they differ in the way they respond to the loss. The pattern and intensity of their grief is unique. It can be hard to acknowledge others' sadness as equally valid or as hard to bear as your own. If you are able to allow for differences, this is helpful for all concerned.

The family has to adjust to filling the gaping chasm left after a death. The deceased might have been the main breadwinner, in which case there are likely to be financial implications. Alternatively, the family's emotional anchor might have been lost, leaving the others uncertain as to whom to turn to in this crisis. To compensate for a loss within the family, individuals are inclined to quickly reform their roles. The eldest son may take on some of the responsibilities his father used to carry. A child might have to look after younger siblings, or a parent may step into a more caring or practical role when a partner dies.

After any kind of disaster, families usually draw closely together. In the case of a death by suicide though, the impact can be powerful enough to undermine their relationships. There are occasions when individuals see each other as being responsible for the death. There may be bitter recriminations of 'you drove him to it', or 'you should have noticed something was wrong'. Feelings of anger and resentment often gnaw away at trust, allowing family rifts to widen. Close relatives probably need mutual support after the death, but they may be too preoccupied with their own distress to be able to reach out to each other. Although it can be difficult to be sensitive to others, it's important to try to survive together through sharing sadness, fears and hopes.

Death as release

Even when the relationship between you and the deceased was unhappy, the loss can be overwhelming. If you had endured abuse from your parent, spouse or partner, it would not be surprising if the death was liberating for you. However, although you might have expressed great relief that the abusive treatment had ended, feelings towards the perpetrator are often ambivalent. The complex nature of the relationship is likely to induce a sense of guilt, especially if you also had some positive and loving memories of the person. This combination of grief and deliverance can lead to self-blame, remorse and unresolved feelings. In general, if you didn't have a secure and trusting relationship with the person before the death, you may find it more difficult to grieve.

It's not abnormal to experience a sense of relief even after the death of a child. The individual and other members of the family may have been deeply unhappy before the death. You could feel relieved if you've been living with your child's previous suicidal behaviour for some time. The repeated threats and the panic visits to the emergency department are physically and emotionally exhausting and can take over your existence. Alternatively, your son or daughter may have suffered mental or physical illness over the years and you might feel relieved that their pain has now ended.

A silent collusion

In the aftermath of suicide, relatives can be unwilling to admit what happened and so try to shroud the death in secrecy. They may be reluctant to discuss either the suicide or the individual who died, so they always keep the conversation on safe ground. The truth becomes vague or distorted and this strategy only offers a short-term solution to coping with painful emotions. Some relatives eventually come to believe that the suicide was really an accident or a natural death. Those not party to the facts are likely to realize that *something* is being kept back and can feel angry and excluded. It's possible there were other suicides in the family in the past. If so, relatives may keep the truth from subsequent generations to spare them the fear of suicide 'running in the family'.

Some families withhold the real cause of death from the outside world. After all, the majority of people who take their own lives are deeply unhappy, and their relatives might worry that it will reflect badly on those left behind. Few of us want our family problems to come under public scrutiny, especially where there is a history of alcohol or drug misuse, debt or sexual difficulties. Regrettably, though, this creates an atmosphere of 'us and them' that can drive a wedge between the family and sources of external support. On occasion, relatives are relieved when the truth comes out, as this gives them a chance to seek help and reassurance.

Losing your child

Many say the most daunting bereavement to face is the loss of a child. You have a natural expectation that your children will outlive you. The fact that your daughter or son killed themselves magnifies the anguish and their act can seem like a blunt rejection of you as a parent. You could feel guilty that you're still alive or even think about your own suicide as a way out of the despair.

Why were they so desperate that they took such a radical step? This question surely haunts every parent whose child has taken his or her own life. You churn over past events in your mind, searching for clues that will unravel the mystery and answer the impossible questions. So many parents ask, 'What's wrong with us?', or 'Did we contribute to our son's state of mind, his personality, or this final act of self-destruction?' You've probably already discovered how many thoughts there are to torture yourself with, and could perhaps think that it only happened because you made some terrible mistakes. You believe it's an integral part of your role to protect your child and you worry that you've failed to understand their problems, to comfort them or make them happy. However, it's important to keep in mind that there's no such thing as an ideal parent and that you are not the cause of your son's or daughter's death.

Lisa's son David was 16 when he jumped from a bridge on the M6 motorway into the path of a petrol tanker. His action totally bewildered his mother. 'He was doing well at school and had everything to look forward to. He'd even saved the money to go on holiday to Corsica with his mates in the summer. I used to lie awake at night asking myself why he did it.' One of David's friends said he'd been depressed about a split with his girlfriend earlier that year. This revelation shocked Lisa. 'We didn't know his relationship was that serious. I was his mother and I *should* have known something was wrong. I'll always blame myself for his death.' As well as feeling guilty, she was anxious that others would judge her as an unworthy parent. 'A few of my friends reinforced my fear that the suicide was my fault. They implied that I didn't have a good enough relationship with David.' It took Lisa many months to realize the truth. David had been depressed and had successfully concealed it from his parents. Lisa wasn't the cause of her son's death, and the guilt she felt was actually a symptom of her grief.

Whether you had a good or difficult relationship with your son or daughter, you will face distressing and sometimes conflicting emotions after the death. If you have other children, the suicide can undermine your confidence in bringing them up. It's important to resist the temptation to see yourself as a failed parent, as they really do need your support now. It might be good to enlist some help from relatives until your confidence returns. It also isn't unusual to find yourself worrying that your other children may be vulnerable to suicide. If you are aware of your fears, you are less likely to become overprotective. You may feel desperate to prove to yourself and the world that you're still a good parent. There's nothing wrong with feeling that way, although you do need to be careful that you don't inadvertently put pressure on your child to be happy, successful, or perfectly behaved.

In trying to cheer you up, others sometimes try to reassure you that you're lucky to have one or more children still alive. This can be very painful, and you know that nothing can replace your child and the fact that you have, or could have, other children doesn't lessen your grief. It's relatively uncommon to have to endure the death of a child, so you need to remember that others are struggling to get it right and will sometimes end up saying the wrong thing.

If you've suffered the death of an only child, you suddenly become childless. Your role as a parent meets a cruel and abrupt end and your world can seem empty and pointless. You might ask yourself whether you're still a parent. Most certainly, you are, and you'll *always* be one. You are the guardian of the memories of your child and they will live on as part of you.

The grief of parents is intense and prolonged, and mother and father often mourn in different ways. They sometimes feel that the grief stretches their relationship beyond its limits. This can be a consequence of:

- Being unable to share feelings about the death.
- Finding it unbearable to be with each other's pain.
- Thinking the other parent is to blame for the suicide.
- Recognizing their reasons for staying together have changed or dissolved.

Sadly, it's not unusual for parents to separate after the tragedy of a child's death. In the United States, as many as 70 per cent of parents of teenagers who commit suicide eventually divorce.

Emily's parents lost their only daughter to suicide:

We didn't talk for months after Emily died and were unable to share our deepest fears. In the end, we went for relationship counselling and discovered that our perception of the suicide was entirely different. When our daughter died, my wife lost the companion and confidante she thought Emily would have been to her in future years. I hadn't considered the future, and just felt stunned and angry at losing my little girl. The difference in our grieving opened up a huge rift between us that we just couldn't reconcile.

This is a heartbreaking story, but such troubles aren't inevitable. Some parents have been able to express their true feelings about the

63

suicide and have become closer to each other as they work through their mutual sorrow. Whether or not you have a spouse or partner to share your loss with, you may feel terribly vulnerable. It's vital to focus on your future survival and the positive things in your life. It may help if you can take comfort from the memories you hold of your child. These are now an essential part of you, and will remain with you for ever.

Losing an adult child

Bereavement through suicide is shocking and painful regardless of the age of your child. Even if they've reached the age of 50 or more, the news is just as devastating. You've had a long time to develop an ongoing and mature relationship, and you may be losing a friend as well as a son or daughter. When they die you lose an essential connection with both your past and your future. You may feel you have nothing to live for. People often assume that losing an adult child is less painful, so they don't acknowledge your heartache.

If your child is married, the focus of compassion is usually on the partner and the children, rather than on you as the parent.

> Graeme's 34-year-old daughter Rosie took her own life after a miscarriage. She left a nine-year-old son, Josh. The family had done everything they could to support her and her husband before she died. 'Rosie was our only daughter and she was very precious to us. We were all worried about Josh after losing his mum and he came to stay with us for a few weeks. Once he went back to his dad, no one else in the family seemed to realize how tormented we were over the tragedy.' Graeme and his wife found the support of understanding friends invaluable in helping them to cope with their loss. They also realized that many parents had been through the experience of losing their adult child, and in time the wounds did begin to heal.

Losing a parent

As a child, the effect of the suicide of your mum or dad can be shattering. You have a unique relationship with your parents. They teach you how to eat, dress and communicate. They help you to develop a sense of identity and worth. It's hardly surprising that the bond is special, as your earliest memories stem from this primary attachment. You will probably recall both the happy and sad occasions as well as times when they comforted and reassured you. After the death, you grieve for your mum or dad, but you also miss all the things that as a parent they used to provide for you.

You depend on your parents to be there, and when one of them dies you may feel sad, frightened and abandoned. Kiran's dad hung himself 15 years ago when she was eight:

> I thought it was my fault because I'd lost a scarf my aunt gave me for my birthday. He was angry that I could have been so careless. After he died, I dreamed that I had to find the scarf, or something terrible would happen. Then I'd wake up in the morning and realized the awful thing had already happened. He was dead. My mum told me he was very unhappy, and that he couldn't stay with us any more. I felt very hurt that he didn't think we were worth living for. I think the grief overwhelmed my mum and she never mentioned him again. I felt as though she'd deserted me as well.

Adults don't always tell children the truth about how their parent died, and this can leave them feeling puzzled and left out. They pick up the distress of adults around them and it's inevitable they'll recognize that others know more than they do. These days, thankfully, it's more likely that children will be trusted to deal with the truth. A young child, however, needs things explained in very simple terms, and adults can give them the full picture as they get older.

Children are often conscious of having to 'grow up' abruptly in response to the loss. This implies that, in addition to mourning the parent's death, there is a need to mourn the loss of childhood or youth. When I was told of my mum's death, my known world crashed to a halt. I knew in my heart that this was a monumental event. It would transform my life and I would never fully recover from the loss. There is one thing I remember vividly. Now that Mum was dead, I couldn't imagine indulging in childish things. Later that week I was astonished when my aunt suggested I go out to play with friends. I couldn't believe she still saw me as a child, and considered it appropriate for me to 'play' when I had no mother! My situation and outlook had changed in a profound and immeasurable way.

Child survivors often don't become aware of the true repercussions of the suicide until much later. If you lost your parent when you were a child, some aspects of the death may continue to haunt you. You'll have gone through a number of developmental stages from childhood and the teenage years into young adulthood. Your perception of the death and feelings of grief are likely to have changed as you integrated the loss into your developing understanding. The suicide will always be a part of your experience and make-up, and you may want to re-examine what happened. Normal grieving can continue until you reach the age of 18 or more. There's evidence to suggest that the death of a parent during childhood sometimes contributes to depression and an increased risk of suicide in later life.

Losing a parent when you are adult

You tend to see your parents as being somehow immortal. Usually your relationship with them persists beyond simply meeting your survival needs as an infant or child. Some describe the influence of their parents as a vital artery that sustains their very existence. The closeness develops over many years and tolerates challenging circumstances and events. You know, of course, that they will die one day, but you push the thoughts from your mind. It's much easier to believe that nothing will ever happen to them. Whatever age you are when they die, the impact of the loss can be tremendous. You may have been in close contact with your mum or dad, or not seen them for many years. The death is likely to be significant even if they didn't have a central role in your adult life.

If you have a surviving parent, your relationship with them will almost certainly change. Your struggle to deal with the loss tends to highlight the nature of your relationship and how well you got on. Following the death of your parent, you have to deal with your other parent's grief in addition to your own. There could also be recriminations within the family over the reasons for the suicide that may put a strain on relationships. You may feel a step closer to your own death, especially if it's your last parent who has died. There's no longer anyone standing as the guardian between you and your ultimate death. You may find it quite a shock to realize that you're technically an orphan, and you can feel alone and defenceless. The death represents the final loss of your childhood and your family history. As an adult son or daughter, you might feel people expect you to get over the suicide very quickly, but the mourning for such a significant loss takes time.

Losing a brother or sister

When you lose a sibling to suicide, others may fail to acknowledge your pain and distress, leaving you feeling neglected. It's easy to underestimate the special bond between brothers and sisters, and some refer to these close survivors as the 'forgotten mourners'. If you grew up together, in all probability you shared many things, including a bedroom, holidays, happy times and disasters. You may have been good companions and stood by each other when things were difficult. There may also have been some rivalry between you, leading to mixed feelings of love and jealousy. The suicide can lead to ambivalent feelings of loneliness, guilt, or even relief. You could feel guilty about any part you think you played in this misfortune, particularly if your younger brother or sister has died. Grief for their son or daughter may overwhelm your parents to the extent that they can't help or encourage you.

When Will was 11 his teenage sister took an overdose. 'My life changed totally when Sara died. We didn't celebrate Christmas or go on holiday for the next two years. I thought that because Sara wasn't alive and happy, we weren't allowed to be happy either. I was crushed by the pain and couldn't cope with my mum's and dad's obsession with her death.' For years, Will was angry with his parents and Sara for leaving him in such an impossible situation. Although she was dead, Sara received all the attention, and he felt ignored and unimportant. He now understands what his parents had been going through, but he still feels he lost a significant part of his childhood.

Fortunately, it isn't always that way and others may have found that the suicide brought the family closer together. As a brother or sister, you could have received the help and reinforcement you needed in your grieving.

The parents may idealize their dead child, creating impossibly high expectations for surviving brothers and sisters. Life can be particularly difficult when you are the only child left to make up for your parents' loss and disappointment. The onus could suddenly be on you to be everything to your parents. You probably still feel that you couldn't ever live up to such a towering expectation and may be resentful about the responsibility you inherited. Your life is entirely separate from your brother's or sister's. You can't possibly make up for such an enormous tragedy and your parents shouldn't expect you to.

Whatever kind of relationship you share as children or adults, the bond between siblings remains until death. Your brother or sister is irreplaceable, and it's important that your grief is recognized by others.

Losing your spouse or partner

Whether you've been together with your loved one for a few short weeks or 50 years, their suicide can leave you with a frightful sense of rejection and inadequacy. You might feel that your partner deprived you of the chance to understand or share their problem. Their suicide meant you had no chance to say goodbye. You're likely to feel very fragile, with no one you can depend on to look out for your interests now.

Beverley's husband Ian drowned himself in the river 15 miles away from their home. He had been made redundant from work, and his mother's recent death sent him into a downward spiral of depression. The police called at 7 a.m. with the news. 'I simply disintegrated. I didn't know who or where I was in those first few days. I hit out at the police officer when she asked if Ian and I had argued before he left the house. Then I cried for days. For the first five months after his death I couldn't bear the time I spent alone. The worst thing was waking up in the early hours of the morning to find I was in an empty bed. We'd lived together for 27 years and I couldn't see an end to the terrible loneliness. I felt as though he'd left me to live my life in torment.' Beverley had reached her lowest point since Ian's death. 'I remember thinking that's it now, I can't possibly feel any worse. That made me realize I was allowing my life to slip away from me and I decided it was time to talk about my grief and begin to accept it.'

You could feel abandoned after the suicide of someone so very close to you. It's hard to escape the notion that they chose death over living with you. Everyone who has lost a spouse or partner through suicide asks themselves what they could have done to prevent such a sad end to their most precious relationship. But did your partner really decide to leave *you*? Or were they leaving themselves and escaping their pain? You must remember that the person almost certainly felt they didn't have a choice: they simply had to flee their misery. Also, it's more than likely they were unable to comprehend that you cared about them. Those who have made a suicide attempt that didn't result in death recall that at the time they were totally preoccupied with their own feelings. They rarely thought of anyone else except in the context of, 'They'll be better off without me.' As one woman said: 'I truly believed I was doing my husband a favour by getting myself out of his life. It's only now I can see he didn't want that. If I'd let myself think about the pain it would cause him, I couldn't have done it.'

Society seems to regard a husband or wife as the major influence on the happiness and well-being of their partner. You may even perceive yourself as having failed to make the relationship work. It's not uncommon for in-laws and the surviving spouse to fall out after a suicide. Beverley was distraught when her husband's parents questioned her about her job and commented that she hadn't spent enough time at home: 'I'm convinced they thought it was all my fault, as I obviously couldn't make him happy enough to want to live.' It's possible that both the partner and the parents are struggling to come to terms with their own anguish and so look for someone else to blame for the tragedy. When this happens it's crucial that you don't feel guilty and that you look for encouragement from your own family or trusted friends. Try not to drift into the trap of believing that you were in control of your partner's happiness, health or outlook on the world. Although you were in a partnership, you aren't to blame for the death, and it was your partner, not you, who took the fatal decision.

Non-married partners may not have any control over decisions made about the body or the funeral, as these responsibilities legally belong to the individual's next of kin. This may generate disagreements with your partner's family and cause further unhappiness for you. Ideally, as a surviving partner, you and the family will be able to work together to make the decisions that you feel are important.

Gay and lesbian partners

Gay and lesbian partners are often the hidden survivors of a suicide. As a couple you may have been discreet about your relationship and kept it from family or friends. The facts are likely to become public knowledge at the inquest, exposing your relationship at a time when you're still reeling from the loss. In common with other non-married partners, you will not be regarded as the person's next of kin, even if it had been a long-standing relationship.

You're likely to have had a closer relationship with your loved one than their relatives had, but gay or lesbian partners may be given little or no support. The family might have been aware of the relationship, but refused to accept or acknowledge its significance.

When his partner of ten years died, Martin found that the reactions of others made grieving difficult: 'They treated me as though I had lost a friend, rather than a lifelong partner and lover. It devalued our relationship and the immensity of the loss. Consequently, people expected me to get over his death within a few months.' Not only is the suicide a tremendous blow, but you may also have to deal with it in relative isolation.

Other people, including the family, can be quick to assume that either the person killed themselves *because* they were gay, or that they had HIV/AIDS. This leaves you to cope with the legacy of speculation about the motivation for the suicide and the possibility of discrimination in seeking help. Above all, you need to keep it in mind that you are facing unjust disadvantages. You may not know which way to turn for comfort, but it's important to seek out help so that your grief doesn't leave you stranded. If your own family or friends are unable to offer you understanding and support, you may wish to contact the Lesbian and Gay Bereavement Project. The contact number is listed in the Useful Addresses section at the back of this book.

Suicide of a friend

We choose our friends and often confide in them more than in our family, so it could be a close friend who is most intimately involved with the suicide. You may have been the only person who was aware of the threat, or had some insight into your friend's state of mind. It's possible you were the one who received a call for help or discovered the body. If you've lost a special friend, the experience can be just as traumatic as for the individual's relatives. Consequently, it's helpful when others are able to perceive you as a survivor with your own need for support and consolation. You might want to share the loss and grief with the individual's family, but this isn't always an option.

The suicide of any acquaintance can be deeply disturbing, even if you weren't especially close. Many years ago, I was friendly with a work colleague who jumped to her death from a bridge. I discovered afterwards that she'd been depressed and was taking prescribed barbiturates. The violent way she died somehow drew me into her world. I agonized over what I imagined her last few weeks had been like and why her life had ultimately become unbearable. I was upset that I hadn't been aware that her depression was so severe. I wondered if I should have noticed, or if there was anything I could have done to prevent her from dying such a lonely death. Hindsight always comes too late, and although I gave myself a hard time over her suicide, I've had to accept that I'll never know whether the outcome could have been different.

Losing a client

People in the caring professions – such as doctors, psychiatric staff or counsellors – frequently have to deal with the suicide of a patient or client. The individual may have been ill, depressed or bereaved and you may have developed a long-term or intense therapeutic relationship with them. Your role is to help and support the individual, so if they kill themselves, you can feel you've completely failed. Others could judge you as having been in an ideal position to predict the suicide, yet were unable to do so. Consequently, you suffer both guilt and anger and may hold yourself responsible. It's vital to seek help from a supervisor or manager to deal with the personal and professional issues this raises. Regardless of the amount of work done by helpers in a statutory or voluntary capacity, a number of people will commit suicide. You can offer understanding, treatment and support, but you can't stop someone taking his or her own life. You need to recognize that it's out of your control.

Summary

- Suicide affects a wide circle of people, all of whom react in different ways.
- The family often colludes in covering up the cause of death or the reason for the suicide. The secrets may be kept from other family members or from the outside world.
- Family members are usually able to assist one another in recovery if they acknowledge their differing feelings and needs.
- A suicide can be equally distressing for friends, colleagues and helpers.
- Individuals who take their own lives usually do so in order to avoid their continuing pain. They may not have realized how much pain their action would cause you.
- People are in charge of their own happiness and you are not responsible for their death.

8

A Special Grief

Although most survivors experience a period of denial following the death, the reality begins to sink in over the weeks and months. The length of time this takes varies widely, and some continue to suffer from sporadic pangs of disbelief years after the event. When you maintain denial of what's happened, however, you can hold up the progress of your recovery. You might already have accepted the reality, but still feel depressed or engrossed in the loss. Although millions of people have been through it and you are not alone, the circumstances of your loved one's death are unique. You may have a number of symptoms in common with other survivors, but ultimately you will deal with the loss in your own way.

A life sentence?

Some people have described suicide as a life sentence imposed by the deceased. It places a formidable burden on you and compels you to face up to deep-seated fears. You have to cope not only with the loss, but also with the disquiet about your own role in the death. You wrestle with trying to understand the reasons for the suicide by asking yourself endless questions. As the circumstances of the disaster unfold, what you discover might be sad, horrific or inexplicable. After the death of a loved one, nothing is ever the same. Although unfortunately there are no short-cuts to healing, your grief doesn't have to be a life sentence. Your symptoms may be severe and bewildering, but they will subside, even if it doesn't seem like it now.

Getting through each day

The overwhelming grief after suicide can make you wonder how you're going to survive without your loved one over the coming weeks and months. For the time being, try not to worry about what lies ahead, but concentrate instead on getting yourself through today.

Any survivor will tell you that it isn't easy to keep going, but you are doing just that. Right now, that's all you need to aim for – getting through each day. Tomorrow will come in any case, and you will deal with that when it comes. In time, the days *will* get easier for you.

A *host of symptoms*

Once the initial shock wears off, the enormity of the loss begins to set in. Grief unleashes numerous symptoms and, like the contents of Pandora's box, once they're out you can feel as though everything is out of control.

Common physical symptoms
- Nervousness or trembling.
- Breathlessness.
- Crying.
- Exhaustion.
- Hollow stomach or nausea.
- Insomnia, or sleeping too much.
- Restlessness.

Common psychological symptoms
- Shock and disbelief.
- Anger and frustration.
- Irritability.
- Depression.
- Disturbed dreams.
- Fear or panic.
- Preoccupation.
- Guilt.
- Relief or elation.

It's easy to think you're going crazy, but all of the above are normal and understandable reactions after bereavement.

Sadness

As our emotions tend to be close to the surface, they can emerge unexpectedly. Something you see, hear or think about may trigger a sorrowful reaction. This could feel like a punch in the stomach and make you feel sick or tearful. You could be sitting on a bus, walking around the shopping mall, or socializing with friends. Crying can be a way of releasing stress, so you may come to regard your tears as a comfort and a friend. After the search party dragged Beverley's husband from the river, she began a period of almost constant weeping. 'Whenever I thought about Ian I burst into tears. I was embarrassed to start with and afraid that people would think I was silly or losing my mind. After a while I accepted it and let the tears flow whenever I felt sad.' Of course, not everyone wants to cry and this is also a normal response after loss.

Depression

There is a difference between the sadness of grief and a longer-term state of depression. If your desperate feelings persist, or you experience suicidal thoughts yourself, it could very well be a sign of depression. Unfortunately, it's easy to be depressed without realizing it, and so it may take a long time before you seek help. There are no magic cures. Treatment with drugs can ease you through a crisis, but it's more effective when used in conjunction with counselling or other therapies. If your doctor prescribes anti-depressants, it's essential to give them time to work. Most take between two and six weeks before you start to feel the benefits, but many people give up after a few days because they don't feel any better. Medication is not going to solve problems or do the grieving for you. If you're deeply depressed, however, it can make an enormous difference to how you feel and help to restore your perspective. Feeling hopeless, for example, is a common symptom of the illness. With treatment, you can see that it was a symptom of depression, rather than that your situation was actually without hope. As Phil discovered, 'The thoughts about taking my own life that surfaced uncontrollably made things seem intolerable. I was shocked when my doctor told me I was depressed and, to be honest, I didn't really believe him. After some weeks on medication, however, I suddenly realized that my illness rather than my circumstances had caused the suicidal thoughts.'

Fear and abandonment

After a significant loss, there are always things to make you anxious and afraid. The stress you're under contributes to your vulnerability. Things you might feel afraid of include:

75

- Dying yourself.
- Losing another close relative or friend.
- Being lonely.
- Sleeping in the house alone.
- Raising children on your own.
- Driving alone.
- Losing your home.

The first step in managing your fears is to identify what they are, and note what specific events or situations you are worried about. Try writing them down and remember that you don't have to show these to anyone else. For instance, if you are afraid of sleeping in the house on your own, list the reasons why. Maybe you think the security is poor and that someone will break in; or that you'll forget to turn off the gas fire when you go to bed. Then think about whether you can do anything about these things to make you feel less anxious. You could have a new lock or alarm fitted, or have a checklist of things you need to do last thing at night. The reality is often not as frightening as you think it's going to be.

Anger

Anger normally arises from feelings of frustration and is natural after any bereavement, but particularly after suicide. It can distort our perceptions and separate us from the real cause of our rage. You may be angry if you believe the person you loved took his or her own life to punish you for something you did or didn't do. The fact that they punished you in a way that the entire world could see makes it seem far worse. You may feel furious at being deserted or betrayed by them. Although it may not be appropriate to display your rage, it's generally best to acknowledge that you do feel angry.

Most of us express feelings of unfairness when we encounter misfortune. You may think that it shouldn't happen to you, and that neither you nor your loved one deserved it. When the suicide defies explanation, it's easy to feel rage towards an external force, or fate. You want to believe that life is fair, but sadly that's not the way things work out. Sometimes tragedies just happen and the individuals we love the most do the unexpected. The shock of the death and perplexing thoughts can lead to ambivalent emotions. These might include an uncomfortable mixture of anger, blame and guilt.

A question of guilt and blame

When an individual takes their own life, family or friends are the first people to come under scrutiny. Others, including the press, tend to look for a reason for the suicide, or even for a guilty party who is directly responsible. There is often the assumption that something must have driven the individual to it.

Beverley was horrified when the local newspaper ran a story after her husband drowned himself. The wording implied that despite Ian's recent redundancy, it was marriage problems that led to his suicide. All her neighbours knew about it. 'I thought they were staring at me as though I was some kind of monster. I was sure people were saying things like "Why didn't she help him?" and "How could she have let this happen?" '

Blaming others

If our first instinct after a suicide is to look for someone to blame, there may be a convenient target within the family. To have your family regard you as the cause of all its problems is a hefty burden that no individual should have to shoulder. Often, though, relatives are more inclined to criticize psychiatrists, doctors or social workers for failing to prevent the death. Unfortunately, suicide is rarely a predictable act and, although blaming is a spontaneous reaction, it isn't rational or fair to assign the liability to individuals.

Blaming the individual

If someone you cared about had been murdered you'd be likely to feel rage towards the perpetrator. With suicide, we know the killer's identity, but how do we justify being angry with the killer when they are also the person who died? We often do feel angry, and the dilemma of caring about our loved one and hating the killer can be disturbing. You feel angry and upset that they came to their decision without seeking help or consulting you.

Jake, whose wife took an overdose, said, 'I still can't believe it. We had some financial problems I know, but she didn't need to go this far. I honestly thought we shared everything and solved problems together. This time, she really left me out in the cold and I resent her decision.' Jake later came to appreciate that his

77

wife was in such an emotional state at the time of her death that she was unable to act as she normally would.

Blaming yourself

Grief after suicide may be characterized by overwhelming feelings of guilt and responsibility. We're inclined to judge ourselves more harshly than others do. However, there's an important difference between recognizing where problems existed and blaming yourself for the death. Looked at objectively, the guilt is emotional rather than rational. Thinking you might be accountable for the suicide is one method your mind uses to deal with this unwelcome situation. You need to decide how to cope with the apparent guilt and your response to the suicide. One way of working through this is to consider what you'd hoped for at the time. If you had a fierce argument or fell out with the person before they died, what was your true intention? Perhaps you just wanted to protect your child, or end a difficult or painful relationship with a lover. You could have been feeling ill, or were in a bad mood. You might think that the suicide was your fault, but things are never that simple. It's certain you didn't intend your actions to hurt the person so deeply that they would kill themselves. Taking a more realistic perspective won't bring the person back, but it can help you to accept that what *they* did wasn't *your* fault. You may find it empowering to take some control of your thoughts:

- Refuse to feel responsible for other people's actions.
- Try not to blame yourself illogically.
- Accept that it's natural to be sad or upset.
- Realize that the feelings of guilt serve no purpose.

Sometimes we make the people we care about unhappy, but this alone does not lead them to the brink of suicide. 'If only I'd had another baby', 'If only I hadn't left home', 'If only I had kept up the mortgage'. None of us is perfect. *The willingness to understand and forgive your own past behaviour is an important step in recovering from the trauma.*

If the reasons for the suicide are apparent, you're less likely to feel guilty. If the individual was chronically sick or suffering from mental illness, for example, it may be easier for you to accept that it was their particular circumstances that contributed to their decision.

Remembering the real person

Bereaved relatives sometimes idealize the loved one who died. Whether husband or wife, child or parent, it's tempting to remember only the good things about them. 'She was beautiful and so clever' or 'He was always such a good son'. We also have the saying, 'You mustn't think ill of the dead', so often we try not to dwell on the person's shortcomings. It's good, however, to have a more realistic image of what people were like, and perhaps recall they could also be lazy, selfish, dishonest or bad-tempered. Survivors are sometimes trapped in their mourning by the memory of the perfect child, parent or spouse.

Mourning and recovery

You may have come across the idea of different 'stages of grief' which describe some of the common symptoms of the mourning process. Not everyone finds this approach helpful, and some are anxious that they have to pass through the various stages of anger and guilt in a precise sequence. A useful guide is Worden's four 'tasks' of mourning, all of which you will work through over time. There is no prescribed order of tasks to be completed, and if you get through each day you will gradually adjust to your new circumstances.

1 Accepting the reality of the loss

This means realizing that the person won't ever come back and recognizing the meaning of what you've lost. Sometimes people deny the importance of the loss in their life and may say, 'I've hardly noticed he's gone' or 'We never got on very well'.

2 Working through the pain of grief

All of us experience some degree of pain after loss. You must allow yourself the time and space to have natural feelings of grief and sorrow.

3 *Learning to live without the person*

At some point you'll need to come to terms with your circumstances and take on new roles. This may involve living alone, raising children as a single parent, or being an only child.

4 *Moving on with life*

Eventually you have to withdraw your emotional investment and redefine your relationship with your loved one in a way that doesn't interfere with you living your life. Although you are essentially the same person as you were before the death, you can only get through the loss by adapting to a different future without them.

Preoccupation with the death

Occasionally an individual, or indeed the whole family, becomes immersed in the death and withdraws into a perpetual state of grieving. They visit the grave every day, or create a shrine to their child or spouse. In the early stages of grief it's normal to spend all your time thinking about the death and the circumstances that led up to it. Sometimes the struggle to understand the reasons for the suicide and the feelings of your loved one before their death can take over your existence. If thinking about the suicide is your only or main activity, it isn't healthy for you or others. It helps to be aware of this danger as it may lead to unresolved grief.

Normal and unresolved grief

If you're stuck in your grieving and things aren't moving on, it's like having your wheels slipping in the mud. You get frustrated and make no progress, or even feel as though you're going backwards. Occasionally people feel worse after a year or two than they did in the initial months after the death. This may be grief that is unresolved and it can follow suicide, particularly if:

- You witnessed the suicide.
- The death was violent or traumatic.
- You've suffered other losses that are still painful.

- You have little or no family support.
- You had 'unfinished business' with your loved one, such as an argument that was never settled.

Although it's important not to put a time limit on the length of your grieving, you may feel worried if it seems endless. At some point, you'll want to move on and follow up new activities rather than the central fact of your existence being that you've lived through a suicide. If you choose to go on identifying yourself primarily as a 'survivor', you could find it hard to appreciate other areas of your life. When your reactions to the suicide consume you, it's easy to blame all of life's problems on this one misfortune. However, your life is extremely complex and this perspective only serves to mask other problems that need tackling in a different way. If your agony doesn't lessen over a period of one to two years, and your approach to recovery doesn't seem to be working, you probably need a new strategy. Do think about getting some help if you're concerned that you're not making any progress in healing your deep wounds. You have a life to live.

Although it might seem strange, people sometimes, consciously or unconsciously, don't want to get better. The suicide and their grief take them over and they can't imagine how they would survive without having it to cling on to. Don't let this happen to you! It is incredibly hard, but you must resist the temptation to reside in the comparative safety and comfort of your grief. In the same way that your loved one was responsible for their decision to die, so your own recovery depends on *you* and not on anyone else. You could chart your own progress over the first one or two years, perhaps by keeping a journal. This will help you to identify the changes you make and understand your grieving as a journey.

When children grieve

Coping with a suicide is a daunting enough task for adults. Sharing your pain with little ones is a difficult but achievable undertaking. Children have the same emotional needs after such a loss, yet adults don't always treat their sorrow as seriously as it deserves. Their grief is often intermittent and they are able to get lost in their games and activities for a while, playing happily one minute and then getting very upset the next.

Children experience a wide range of upsetting emotions. Usually their bereavement will mean a separation from a parent, brother, sister or grandparent. Little ones see themselves as the centre of their own world, so when a disaster occurs they may think it's their fault: 'I must have done something wrong to make Daddy kill himself.' They need to have it explained to them that it wasn't their fault and that the person did love them.

Not all children display their emotions. Joe was seven when his dad took his own life. His mum was worried about Joe's response to the loss: 'At times, he appears oblivious to the fact that his dad's dead. He never cries or asks questions about him. I must admit I don't understand what's going on in his world.' When a child hides their sadness from adults like Joe did, it's often because they don't know how to behave. It's also possible that they're trying to protect you from their grief and so suppress their real feelings. This can be a worry and their anxiety might emerge later in disturbed behaviour, refusal to go to school, or withdrawal from activities and interests. These reactions are quite common, and not of major concern providing the episodes fade with time. Other signs of anxiety include:

- Refusing to eat.
- Withdrawing from people.
- Hyperactivity.
- Appearing disoriented.

These are all normal expressions of grief. There may be cause for concern when a child appears to be persistently disturbed, demonstrates significant withdrawal behaviour, or displays no emotion at all. These are potential warning signs that may call for professional intervention by the family doctor or more specialist support through a child and family guidance clinic.

Helping bereaved children

Adults in the family have to deal with their own grief, and so may not be able to extend much-needed support to their little ones. Children tend to take their cues from adults as to how to behave in extreme situations, so it's usually a good idea to let them see you display your sorrow and let them cry with you. After a suicide, a child needs reassurance about the past and the future. It is helpful to explain that not everyone who gets ill or depressed will die in this way. It's important to encourage children to express and understand their feelings. The only way to do this is to ask them how they feel and what they're thinking. What, in particular, are they anxious about? You then have a chance to empathize with the way they feel so that they realize that you take their concerns seriously.

If a parent has died, children want to know that their other parent or a significant relative will be there for them. They worry about who will look after them and love them and may fear losing their other parent. Many children are fearful or embarrassed about going back to school. I categorically refused to go to school after my mum's death. Looking back on it now I wonder if it was the only way I could express the cruel injustice I felt at having lost my mother. I must admit, I also dreaded confronting school friends and the questions they would ask. My protest was short-lived and my dad offered enough reassurance to persuade me to return. You can help a child through this difficult stage with a planned approach to their return and by enlisting the help of their friends and teachers. Children are usually less anxious and more able to deal with the loss if they have confidence that their life won't fall apart.

Bereavement brings with it a host of supplementary losses for children, which could include losing their home, shared activities and holidays or living on a reduced family income. It's important to remember the huge impact the suicide has had on all aspects of their lives. It's often helpful to ask children what things they miss since the person died. Other approaches to help them come to terms with their changed situation might be:

- Involving them in the family's grieving and listening to their concerns.
- Talking with them about the family member who has died.
- Trying to maintain as normal a routine as possible to make them feel secure.
- Remembering to inform the school of what's happened so that they are alert to any problems the child may display.
- Maintaining family activities as normally as possible.

- Offering special outings, treats or holidays.
- Trying to resist the temptation to allow children to support you emotionally. They are still children and should not be expected to be responsible for the adults in their lives.

Parents or carers may find it helpful to draw in other people who are able to offer extra support to the child. Other relatives, neighbours, teachers and friends could all have a vital role to play in helping children to cope with their grief.

Summary

- The physical and emotional symptoms of grief often come in waves and we all deal with them in our own way.
- Try to remember that you only have to get through today. If you are patient with yourself, in time your symptoms will recede.
- You may find that others turn away from your distress, perhaps because they simply can't find the right words to say.
- Guilt and blame are common after suicide. It's important for your recovery that you recognize it's illogical to feel responsible for the death.
- Many survivors feel depressed, and if this is persistent or you have suicidal thoughts, you should talk to your doctor.
- Normal symptoms of grief pass with time. Although others can help you through the difficult times, you are responsible for your own healing.
- Children's grief is often just as intense as that of adults. The family can help children to feel able to talk about the loss and come to terms with it.

9
Finding Support

Society often perceives suicide as an unacceptable way to die, and the shame attached to it means that support can be hard to find. You're likely to feel very alone if neighbours or colleagues – or even relatives – seem to avoid you. Of course, if you feel wretched, it could be that you're shying away from social contact, so it becomes a two-way problem. When people do approach you with offers of help, think about accepting if you can. You may need to be prepared for the fact that people are good at rallying round when there's a crisis, but once the funeral is over their enthusiasm can dwindle.

Survivors' needs

Although everyone responds differently to their loss, survivors of suicide usually have some needs in common. These could include wanting:

- Information on suicide.
- Practical help or advice.
- Reassurance.
- Consolation.
- Emotional support.

You probably knew very little about suicide before it entered your life so dramatically. Having access to clear information on suicide helps to introduce a sense of perspective about the death. Family, friends and bereavement organizations all have different things to offer. Many people recover perfectly well on their own after a loss and have no reason to seek outside help. Others, however, find the grievous wounds may only begin to heal with a little help and guidance along the way.

Sharing your feelings

Some people will inevitably see your sorrow as alarming, and so feel too intimidated to approach you. Others may simply not be aware that you need practical or emotional support. Keeping in touch with people is very important in the early months after a loss. Relatives and friends sometimes find it difficult to talk about the suicide, so they leave it up to you to raise the subject. It's probably not that they don't care to ask you about it, but that they just don't know what to say.

Recognizing that other people find it immensely difficult to cope with your grief is essential. Try to be aware of the expectations you have of others, including your relatives and friends. If they are too high, you're increasing your chances of feeling let down. What you mustn't do is see your grief as a sign of weakness, because it isn't.

Sometimes people will try to solve all your problems for you, or want to rescue you from your despair. In the early days, however, you may not want anyone to rescue you, even if that were possible. Other people may try to cheer you up or get you out to social events before you feel ready. Activities such as taking a holiday or buying new clothes might distract you from your pain for a while, but the relief is usually short-lived. You may find that it's one particular person who helps you through the crisis, usually a close friend. You just want someone to listen to you, without your grief overwhelming them. Discussing how you're feeling about the death allows them the chance to offer you comfort and support. At times, you'll understandably want to be alone so it always helps to let friends and relatives know that's what you'd prefer.

Sources of help

Some of the main sources of help include:

- Doctors.
- Counsellors and therapists.
- Mental health services.
- Social workers.
- Clergy and religious or spiritual groups.
- Community agencies.
- Bereavement services.
- Support groups.

No approach is necessarily more effective that any other and what is most important is that it feels right for you. Your doctor is often the first point of contact and it's as well to be open about your feelings and symptoms, especially if you're worried that you might be depressed. Some people find that a combination of informal and professional support is invaluable in coping with the emotional fall-out after suicide.

Barriers to getting help

There are many obstacles to getting help after bereavement by suicide. When others make you feel ashamed or guilty about the death, it can be difficult to face the outside world. You may lack confidence in the ability of medical professionals, especially if you believe they failed your loved one in dealing with their problems when they were alive. Approaching them might not feel like an option, so you may have to change your doctor or find alternative help. Some survivors worry that people will judge them as mentally ill if they contact the health service or seek professional counselling. If you're gay or lesbian, or from a minority ethnic group, you could face barriers of discrimination, although there are now a number of bereavement services working with these groups.

Generally speaking, men are less likely to contact agencies, perhaps because they feel they ought to be able to survive without outside support. Maybe they don't perceive themselves to be in need of help, and so tend to develop their own coping strategies. Women, too, sometimes see themselves as 'copers' and prefer to deal with their grief alone. Sometimes, though, too much coping can wear you down, even if you're used to dealing with challenging or extreme circumstances.

Waiting lists are frequently a problem, and many agencies, in particular those that depend on volunteer staff, may not be able to offer you an appointment for weeks or even months. This is maddening when you feel you need to see someone straight away and you will have to be patient or look for help elsewhere.

When to seek help

There is a world of difference in people's timing in seeking help. Some survivors do so almost immediately after the death while others struggle on unsupported for years. The first professionals you come into contact with are likely to be the police, nurses, doctors, social workers, funeral directors and the clergy.

An integral part of the services of a funeral director is offering advice and care to the relatives left behind. The National Association of Funeral Directors provides a Careline for their members to which clients and their families have 24-hour access. The Careline offers counselling, in addition to advice on inheritance, tax, wills and welfare benefits.

Clergy often have a crucial role to play in caring for bereaved family members. The majority of people still choose to have a church funeral, and clergy receive special training in grief support to enable them to offer both immediate help and longer-term counselling. It doesn't matter if you aren't a regular churchgoer or don't want to talk about religion. They are there to listen and will help you to explore feelings of anger, sadness or guilt after a death. A number of churches now run bereavement support groups.

Many people find that they don't need help until a later stage, when the initial shock and numbness of the suicide has worn off. This is when the searing pain of grief can set in. Survivors who are reluctant or nervous about asking for help may find themselves carrying their grief for many years. If, like me, you lost a parent or a sibling when you were a child, you could reach the point in adulthood where you suddenly realize that you need help. If you haven't fully recovered, it's quite common for another traumatic event to trigger grief from the earlier loss. As a child I didn't grieve adequately for my mum, and I was in my early twenties when my dad died. My world folded in for the second time. I began a long journey of grieving for both my parents and had to confront some difficult feelings about the past. We have to face these feelings, regardless of whether the suicide took place five years ago, or 50 years ago. The best time to seek help is when you feel ready and it's right for you, but certainly try to find it if you're struggling to survive or think you're not getting better.

Support groups

Initially you may feel certain that no one else could have undergone the same terrible experience as you have. The notion that you will ever recover seems like a wild dream. No matter how awful or unbearable your plight, you have to remember that it has happened to others. Many of those who've lived through a suicide have a crucial understanding of what you're going through. When you talk with them, you discover how they coped with their loss and worked towards eventual healing. To discover you're not alone in your experience and feelings is, after all, most reassuring. There are many bereavement support groups available, particularly across the United Kingdom, Europe, United States, Canada, Australia and New Zealand.

Self-help groups

In most self-help bereavement groups, the members share the running of the meetings and activities. All groups are different, but most of them welcome relatives and anyone who has been personally touched by a death, such as a friend or colleague. It's not necessarily important how close you were to the individual who died; what really matters is the intensity of your grief. People are usually reassured to learn that their reactions are normal and that they will feel better than they do in the early days. The group can help you to cope and to alleviate the burden of your loss through sharing experiences and anxieties.

Many people find groups that are specifically for those bereaved by suicide to be the most helpful. Members have personal experience of the extra burden of guilt and anger carried by suicide survivors and this reassures them. Stella attended a suicide support group for parents about four months after her son hanged himself:

People kept saying the word 'suicide'. I felt shocked as we'd avoided using the term at home. It sliced into my brain like a scalpel. All I could do was cry. The group was very kind and helped me through my tears. Now I can use the term 'suicide' to describe the fact of his death, whereas before it acted as an emotional trigger. After Adam died, I thought I was going mad. I needed to talk to someone else who'd been through it. For a change, I wanted to hear someone say 'I do know how you feel' and it would be genuine. The group pulled me through the worst of the crisis. They understood the horror and trauma I'd been through. I soon discovered I wasn't the only person who'd thought about killing myself – in fact, most had. I realized my feelings were normal after all! Their stories moved me deeply and I'll never forget them. After a few weeks it dawned on me that some of my old self still existed, and I did care about tragedies other people had to deal with. The sense of shared compassion is heartening and I formed a strong bond with many of the parents.

You may not be fortunate enough to have a suicide-specific group in your area, so a general bereavement group is probably the next best thing. Alternatively, you could consider the feasibility of setting one up yourself. Some people find the idea of a group depressing and morbid, and imagine that members talk incessantly about death. Of course, people share their feelings, say how things are going, and acknowledge what they're finding difficult. There are tears and sorrow, but often there is also lightness and laughter. These can be essential in helping you to come to terms with your loss.

People do survive the death of their loved one by suicide and often surface from their grief to live fuller lives than ever. Those who've progressed further than you offer living examples of those who are on their way to healing. Each person has to find their own answers and develop ways of dealing with their situation. You might not be used to revealing your feelings in front of strangers and it can be difficult to begin with. If you feel anxious about it, you could probably take a friend along with you the first time.

Therapist-led groups

Professional therapists or counsellors may offer bereavement groups. They aim to provide a safe environment in which people feel able to share their experiences and work through the pain of their grief. Many of these are advertised locally, or your nearest bereavement service may have a contact list.

The Internet

There are many websites devoted to the topics of suicide and bereavement, which provide access to a wealth of information. Although some sites are excellent, others are dubious, to say the least, so you must use your own judgement. A number offer chat groups for survivors, and there are people who like the anonymity of this form of communication. It's a way of being in touch with other survivors that allows you to feel accepted without involvement or commitment. This isn't always a good thing, however, and it can encourage you to keep your wounds open rather that allowing them to heal. At times, you need others to challenge your views and inconsistencies on your journey to recovery, and maybe only friends and those who have a commitment to you can offer you this.

Counselling and therapy

Relatives and friends aren't always able to offer the right kind of advice and reassurance. In many cases, survivors find it easier to confide in someone outside the family. If you'd like to find a safe place where you can talk and freely express your emotions of hurt, anger and guilt, then counselling might be for you. There may be real benefits in talking to an uninvolved person, as they have no preconceived ideas about you and your family. They offer an objective approach and the skills to help you understand your grief and develop your own coping strategies.

Jake attended a self-help group for a while after his wife Wendy took an overdose:

> I think the group was excellent for most people, but sometimes I felt I needed time to focus on myself. I arranged to see a one-to-one counsellor for six weeks. The sessions were very intensive and I was exhausted for hours afterwards. The counselling really helped me to gain insight into my wife's suicide and my own distressing emotions. Although my recovery was still a slow and painful process, at least I was moving forward. Now I feel less weighed down by my grief and fear.

Therapy or counselling doesn't suit everyone, and in the early days after the loss you may be feeling too raw to get the best out of it. Before deciding on a grief counsellor, it's wise to obtain a list of accredited or approved practitioners from an organization such as the British Association for Counselling and Psychotherapy. Where more than one family member is in need of help, family therapy is a possible option. Your doctor should be able to provide you with relevant local information or make a referral.

Dealing with special occasions

There are critical times in the calendar that are likely to be stressful reminders of your loved one's suicide:

- Birthdays.
- Christmas.
- Anniversary of the death.
- Other anniversaries.
- Holidays.

Usually, it's the period leading up to the significant date that is the most difficult to deal with. If you feel anxious about how you're going to cope on the day, it's wise to plan your time well in advance, so you know what you will be doing and who is going to be with you. Discuss the day with your family beforehand and decide how you'd like to spend it. You may choose to visit the grave, buy flowers, or light a candle to bring the memory of your loved one closer to you. Naturally, the anniversary of the loss arouses profound feelings of sorrow. Some people say that afterwards they've felt a sense of release. Up until the first anniversary, you can always look back to what you were doing the previous year. You've definitely passed a milestone after a year, and your confidence rises when you realize you've managed to get through it. Successive anniversaries will always be a painful reminder for you, but the intensity of the feelings does fade with time.

Naomi desperately misses her daughter Emily after five years:

I dreaded the first birthday after her death. She would have been 22 then. I started crying the day before and continued for three days. Fortunately, I had a very good friend with me, and she allowed me to talk non-stop about my daughter's life and how much I miss her. She meets up with me on Emily's birthday each year and it helps to get me through. It is getting easier each year, but it will always be a significant day in my diary.

Cruse Bereavement Care

Cruse is a voluntary organization that offers help and advice to anyone affected by a death, and those who are trying to support them. They have counselling services across the United Kingdom and offer:

- A chance to share thoughts and anxieties.
- Time to talk to someone with an understanding of the process of grieving.
- Information and a range of useful publications.
- Contact information on bereavement support services.
- Suicide-specific groups in a number of locations.

The Compassionate Friends (TCF)

The Compassionate Friends is an international, non-profit-making organization. It promotes healing through offering understanding, friendship and grief support to parents following the death of a child. It also advises professional workers and friends who are assisting the family.

Shadow of Suicide (SOS) Support Groups

TCF has a network of groups called Shadow of Suicide (SOS), for parents who have lost a child of any age. As a parent, you could never have been prepared for the suicide of your child. Within a group of parents who've experienced losing their child, you can talk about your son or daughter and know that people in the group will understand your feelings. No other parent has lost what you have, and your relationship with your child was unique. You must pick up the pieces of your own life in your own way and your own time. SOS groups are friendly and informal. Although they can't offer easy solutions to your distress, contact with other parents does provide you with some hope for the future. *You are not alone!*

Survivors of Bereavement by Suicide (SOBS)

SOBS is a self-help voluntary organization that has developed a network of support groups that meet on a monthly basis. It aims to put an end to the isolation of those bereaved by suicide, offering both practical and emotional support. SOBS also produces a bereavement pack for suicide survivors and operates a national Helpline.

Finding out more

You will find a list of useful contact numbers at the back of this book (see Useful Addresses section). Your local library, Citizens Advice Bureau or doctor's surgery may be able to provide you with further information about what's available in your area.

Summary

- There are a variety of routes to recovery and you will find your own sense of direction. Not everyone needs support with their grieving, but for others outside help is invaluable.
- Support groups can help you to realize that you're not alone in your despair and that other people do recover from the tragedy of suicide.
- A range of services exists to help, so if you feel you could do with some extra support, you may as well try out what they have to offer.
- A list of agencies including Cruse, TCF and SOBS, is given in the Useful Addresses section at the back of this book.

10
Shaping the Future

When suicide has scarred our lives, perhaps the challenge is to take what lessons we have learned from it and go on to rebuild our future. This can seem like a monumental task and you may just want to give up, or even think about taking your own life, rather than contemplate any act of bravery or transformation. But the harsh reality of your loss compels you to modify your thinking and redefine your existence. Although you will be the same person, you will undergo change and develop new ways of living. I'm not aware of the time when I started to come to terms with the death of my mum. When you look back on today, you probably won't remember when you began to adapt to your loss. The changes take place slowly, and often indiscernibly.

Taking your time

You can only expect to take small steps forward in your recovery after a suicide. At times, you'll feel as though the grief is wrenching you back into its jaws. Numerous things might act as a trigger: a chance remark perhaps, a television drama, or a piece of music that was special to your loved one. More often than not, you'll discover that other people expect you to get over the suicide very quickly. After a few short weeks or months, they think you should have snapped out of it, but there is nothing prescriptive about how or when you should recover. As time passes you will develop the courage and resources to keep going.

Accepting the loss

Loss is at the core of all of life's misery and challenges. No matter how much we try to fend off unwelcome realities, we have to accept that the people we care about will ultimately die. Your ability to cope is related to your past experience of dealing with loss and you need to acknowledge how the death affects your life. As well as losing the person you care about, there are always supplementary losses to face. Things you will miss could include financial security, companionship, intimacy or mutual support and encouragement.

Your personal history of loss

What was the first loss in your life that you remember? It could have been that your cat went missing, or a favourite toy was broken. I still remember the day someone stole my treasured red bike from our back garden and the depth of anger and dismay I felt. The death of a family member is always significant, and the second important event for me was my mum's death. Other kinds of losses you may have experienced include:

- Loss of a pet.
- Loss of friendship.
- Death of a relative or friend.
- Changing schools.
- Divorce or separation.
- Losing your health or abilities.
- Financial loss or bankruptcy.
- Children leaving home.
- Redundancy or retirement.

It's important to consider how you've dealt with previous losses, as this tends to influence your response to subsequent events. Try compiling your 'personal loss history-chart'. List all the major losses that you recall, starting with those from your childhood and working up to the present day. Record your age at the time and add a few notes to describe the effect the loss had on your life and circumstances.

Personal Loss-history Chart		
Age	Who or what did you lose?	How did the loss affect your life?

You may have only a few events to record. The older you are, the more likely it is that you'll have experienced many losses. Use a separate sheet if you need more space. Now consider each entry in turn and record, on a separate sheet of paper, answers to the following questions:

- How did you cope with the loss?
- Who were the most important people in your life at the time?
- Which of these people are still important in your life?
- What were the important things in your life then (such as a job, hobby or interest)?
- Which of these things have remained constant in your life?
- What was it that helped you through the loss? Could it help you again?

97

As you do the exercise, you'll probably realize that you've already lived through a number of painful losses. Although it might not feel like it now, you are also going to survive this one. Suicide tips your world upside down and you feel as though nothing will ever be the same. If you look more closely, you'll probably find that one or two things, or people, have remained as central features of your existence. As I compiled my own answers, it struck me that my brother had been a constant presence for me. He was in my life when my red bike went missing, when Mum and Dad died, and he was there when I got divorced. I am very fortunate that he is still in my life today. It's essential that you recognize the aspects of *your* everyday life that are now different, and those that are the same as before the death occurred. Those people, or things, that remain consistent can offer you an anchor against the sea of despair.

Loss and gain

In the early days, it may seem as if you've lost everything and gained nothing through this unwelcome death. Your life hasn't turned out quite the way you planned; nevertheless you have the opportunity to rediscover some of the pleasures you once enjoyed, plus some new ones. You've lost a loved one and no one can ever replace them. However, you may be surprised to discover there can be some gains on the path to recovery, including an increase in your capacity to empathize with others, to feel compassion, and to forgive. You undoubtedly feel wretched and it's going to be tough, but you can make positive choices that put you firmly in control of your progress.

Everything changed for Graeme when his daughter Rosie ended her life in suicide:

> It's made me stronger because I've survived the rough times and learnt not to criticize myself too much. My wife feels the same and we are both more easy-going about things that don't really matter. Our bedroom ceiling collapsed recently because the roof was leaking and it ruined all the furniture in the room. Before Rosie's death, we'd have regarded it as a disaster, whereas we now just take it in our stride. The past six years have been a long and painful journey to acceptance for us, but I think we've both come out of it as better people.

98

Forgiveness

If you're serious about moving forward you may need to be careful that you don't let harshness, resentment and misery define your existence. Forgiveness isn't easy, but it's crucial that you don't allow your thoughts to control you. If you are able to find it in your heart to forgive your loved one, yourself and others for the suicide, the rewards will be incalculable.

Beverley recalls how she felt after her husband Ian killed himself:

> For ages I couldn't help but feel rage towards him for leaving me on my own. It stopped me thinking rationally and I swore I'd never forgive him. Then one day at the supermarket I was watching a man helping his wife unload their shopping trolley into the car and I remembered what a caring and thoughtful husband Ian had been to me. It was just a beginning, but after that, I was able to forgive him a little more each day.

Choosing to move on

You may have discovered by now that the hope of finding an explanation for the suicide is often the first sacrifice on your road to healing. One day you have to admit that you don't have an answer, or that any answer you do have will be inconclusive. Even if you have a plausible and meaningful reason, it's not going to change reality.

After Jake's wife Wendy killed herself, he spent 18 months looking for definite clues as to her state of mind:

> I just couldn't believe she'd done it! I thought I knew everything about her life. It all seemed like a horrendous mistake. Our financial problems were not serious enough to warrant this reaction and so I was sure there were other things on her mind. For over a year I thought she must have left a note to explain why she was so upset, and we hadn't found it yet. It still makes no sense to me, but I'm starting to trust that she had her reasons and must have felt desperate. I'd have gone crazy if I hadn't given up my search for answers.

The person who died made a choice on the day they took their own life. You have a choice to make now. You could grieve for ever, brooding and tormenting yourself about the suicide, or you could put the inward-looking aspects of your mourning behind you and look to the future. It's crucial to distinguish between what you are and what you are not able to influence in the world. It's terribly upsetting but you can't reach out to your loved one now. You can, however, do much to help yourself and others.

Handling stress

When the funeral and the inquest are over, many people find there is suddenly less to occupy their time. This is a difficult period in the grieving process and it's vital that you take good care of your health and well-being. Following bereavement, it's inevitable you'll suffer from some degree of stress. There are many techniques that you could try for relieving stress, and two options are relaxation and meditation. Even if you've never considered relaxation or meditation before, why not give them a go? You have nothing to lose.

Relaxation and meditation

Relaxation exercises can be effective in reducing stress and returning a sense of balance to your body and mind. It's ideal to learn a technique and then use it regularly until it's become second nature. Choose an exercise that suits you, perhaps from a book or a relaxation class. Even if you can only set aside 15 minutes each day, you'll find it helps you to cope with stress and anxiety.

Meditation is also a popular way of coping with stress. Many people are put off by it, assuming it's weighed down with religious meaning and ritual. Although it is associated with many of the great spiritual traditions, you don't have to hold a particular belief or religious conviction to benefit from the practice. The aim of meditation is to focus your awareness on one particular thing. It's possible to focus on the rhythm of your breathing, sounds, smells, images, or the sensations of 'just sitting'. Meditation allows the continual chattering voices in your head to settle down and encourages clarity of thought. Finding a good meditation book is invaluable, particularly if you're willing to explore different techniques. Alternatively, you may prefer to be taught through a formal meditation class.

Physical exercise

Physical activity brings not only health benefits, but also psychological ones, and many people find it relieves stress and depression. Whether you go swimming, take a walk in the country, mow the lawn, join a gym, or take up a sport, you should notice the positive effects that exercise can have on your mood. Always check your current state of health with your doctor before starting any new exercise programme.

Planning for tomorrow

The concept of 'getting through today' is a powerful tool in overcoming painful events. To make plans for your future might seem to be a contradiction to this idea. It's feasible, however, to have a vision of where you want to get to, yet take the path towards the goal day by day. This means doing only as much as feels right for you. If the suicide occurred at your home, it would be natural for you to want to move away from the scene of the tragedy. Moving house can be incredibly stressful, though, so it isn't always a good idea to rush these things. It's a major decision that you may later regret. In any case, you won't be able to evade the images and reminders of your loss. If possible, wait until you feel stronger before making important and life-changing decisions.

All of us need to plan for the future and, after a suicide, making realistic short-term plans is a way of taking charge of your life. You might find it helpful to make a copy of the following action plan and fill in the things you aim to do in each of the different areas of your life. This is *your* plan and you don't have to show it to anyone if you don't want to.

Action Plan				
Life area	*I want to achieve*	*By when*	*First steps*	*Follow-up*
Home				
Friends				
Health				
Work				
Leisure				

For example, under the life area 'leisure' Jake noted that he wanted to take up photography, something he'd always wanted to do, but could never get started. In the column 'by when' he set a date for the end of October. He listed his two 'first steps' as signing up for a photography course and, of course, buying a camera! As 'follow-up' he identified that he needed to decide what kind of pictures he wanted to take, and how he was going to further his interest.

Try not to set your goals too high, or you'll feel discouraged if you don't meet them. Check on your action plan once a month and see how you're doing. If you haven't made as much progress as you'd like, don't worry! Simply revise and update your chart and make your goals more achievable. You may be able to make small changes quickly, but it may take several years to meet your most significant goals.

Awareness

One of the harsh lessons of loss is that appreciation of what we have today is of paramount importance. Trevor has become more conscious of time slipping by since his wife's suicide: 'My brother said I'd have to live my life for both of us from now on and that's what I try to do. It gives more meaning and purpose to the things I do, even chores like gardening and cleaning.'

Looking back on our relationship with our loved one, we may think of things we would like to have said or done, but didn't get round to. So perhaps there are things we want to say or do in the time we have left to us now. We tend to feel more happy and contented when we make a conscious effort to appreciate others and ourselves.

Reinvesting in life

Before the suicide, your whole existence may have centred on your loved one. The powerful impact he or she had on you remains. It all seems daunting, but now you need to find a way of investing in other things while retaining the special memories. Only you can work towards your future happiness – no one else can do it for you. You need to replace the grief with something new and invest time and energy in different areas of your life. You may have given up activities and interests since the death that you'd like to pick up again. Or you could feel ready to take up a new pursuit. As long as you don't isolate yourself from people who care about you, then you will make progress.

Beverley found that her recovery made her uneasy at first: 'I felt so guilty about going out and enjoying myself again after my husband's suicide. I felt like a traitor. I worried that I might lose him and the special memories by not grieving any more. Now I'm pleased to be living a full life and the way I remember him hasn't changed at all.'

You probably don't feel it's right to enjoy yourself now, but it's perfectly acceptable and exactly what your loved one would have wanted. You need to get on with *your* life. You'll find new strengths will appear that you didn't know you had. In order to face the future you need to believe in yourself and trust that you will recover. It's important for you to keep on living, not only for yourself, but also because other people need you to be around.

Summary

- After a suicide, nothing can ever be the same again. Change is inevitable, as you learn to adjust to life without the person you cared so much about.
- The wounds can be extremely deep and you must try to be patient with your rate of progress.
- Forgiving your loved one, others and yourself is an important step in taking some control over your own healing.
- It's crucial that you look after yourself and acknowledge your own needs and hopes. If you're going to move on with your life, it helps to set yourself some goals and develop an action plan.
- Surviving a suicide brings out hidden strengths in you that light the way to transition and recovery. You will discover a new future for yourself, but only when you have the courage to loosen your grasp on the past.

Further Reading

Boenisch, E., and Haney, C., *The Stress Owners Manual*, Impact, 1996.

Brautigan, I., *You Can't Catch Death: A Daughter's Memoir*, Canongate, 2001.

Curran, D., *Adolescent Suicidal Behaviour*, Taylor & Francis, 1987.

Dass, R., *Journey of Awakening: A Meditator's Guidebook*, Bantam, 1990.

Dunn, M., *The Good Death Guide*, Pathways, 2000.

Finkbeiner, A., *After the Death of a Child: Living with Loss Through the Years*, Free Press 1996.

Gordon, L., *52 Relaxing Rituals*, Chronicle, 1996.

Home Office Leaflet, *The Work of the Coroner*, Dd 112 10/A 1709 RP 7192.

Hoskins, C., *Surviving Your Child's Suicide: A Mother's Story*, Protea, 2000.

Küng, H., *Dying with Dignity: A Plea for Personal Responsibility*, Continuum, 1998.

Lake, Dr T., *Living with Grief*, Sheldon Press, 1984.

Roet, B., *The Confidence to Be Yourself*, Piatkus, 1999.

Shannon, P., *Bereaved by Suicide*, Cruse Bereavement Care, 2000.

Which? Guide to Wills and Probate, Which? Books, 1997.

Wolpert. L., *Malignant Sadness: The Anatomy of Depression*, Faber & Faber, 1999.

Children and grief

Grollman, A., *Talking about Death*, Beacon Press, 1991.

Rubel, B., *But I Didn't Say Goodbye*, Griefwork Center Inc., 1996.

Stickney, D., *Waterbugs and Dragonflies: Explaining Death to Young Children*, Pilgrim/United Church Press, 1997.

Wells, R., *Helping Children Cope with Grief*, Sheldon Press, 1988.

Useful Addresses

United Kingdom

Cruse Bereavement Care
Cruse House
126 Sheen Road
Richmond
Surrey TW9 1UR
Helpline: 0870 167 1677
Website: www.crusebereavementcare.org.uk

Survivors of Bereavement by Suicide (SOBS)
Centre 88
Saner Street
Hull HU3 2TR
Helpline: 0870 241 3337
Website: www.uk-sobs.org.uk

The Compassionate Friends (TCF)
53 North Street
Bristol BS3 1EN
Helpline: 0117 953 9639
Website: www.tcf.org.uk

National Association of Bereavement Services
2nd Floor
4 Pinchin Street
London E1 1SA
Helpline: 020 7709 9090

The Bereavement Counselling Service
Dublin Street
Baldoyle
Dublin 13
Ireland
Tel: 00 353 8391766

ject

n–Fri 7 p.m.–10.30 p.m.

elling Service

Counselling and Psychotherapy

1 2PJ
9
ac.co.uk

r Black Bereaved Families
Square

19 1JE
8661 7228

al Association of Funeral Directors (NAFD)
Warwick Road
olihull
West Midlands B91 1AA
Tel: 0121 711 1343
Website: www.nafd.org.uk

The Samaritans
10 The Grove
Slough SL1 1QP
Helpline: 08457 90 90 90
Website: www.samaritans.org.uk

United States

American Association of Suicidology (AAS)

4201 Connecticut Avenue NW
Washington DC 20008
Tel: (202) 237 2280
Website: www.suicidology.org

The Compassionate Friends (TCF)

PO Box 3696
Oak Brook
Illinois 60522–3696
Tel: (708) 990 0010
Website: www.compassionatefriends.org

National Funeral Directors Association (NFDA)

Brookfield
Wisconsin
Tel: (800) 228 6332
Website: www.nfda.org

Canada

The Compassionate Friends (TCF)

685 William Avenue
Winnipeg
Manitoba R3E 0Z2
Tel: (204) 787 4896
Website: www.compassionatefriends.org

Suicide Bereavement Support Group

Canadian Mental Health Association
648 Huron Street
London
Ontario N5Y 4J8
Tel: (519) 4549 199

Australia

National Association for Loss and Grief (NALAG (Aus) Inc)
2 Angrove Road
Somerton Park
SA 5044
Tel (08) 8294 7811
Website: www.griefaustralia.org.

The Compassionate Friends (TCF)
City West Lotteries House
2 Delhi Street
West Perth 6005
Tel: 9486 8711
Website: www.compassionatefriends.org

New Zealand

The Compassionate Friends (TCF)
Website: www.compassionatefriends.org
e-mail: tcfotago@deepsouth.co.nz

Internet resources

Befrienders International
This site is a gateway to over 1,500 suicide and emotional helplines.
Website: www.suicide-helplines.org

Survivors of Suicide
Information and support for suicide survivors.
Website: www.survivorsofsuicide.com

Parents of Suicide
Parents of Suicide offers an e-mail support group.
Website: www.parentsofsuicide.com

Index

abandonment 14, 69, 75–6
abuse 19, 35
accepting the loss 95–8
access to means 23–4
action plan 101–2
adolescents 27–36
age 19 *see also* youth
alcohol misuse 3, 16, 22–3, 29–30,
    33, 35, 39, 61
ambivalence 2, 28, 60
anger 10, 27, 50, 60, 71, 74–9, 89,
    91–2
anorexia 30
antidepressants 42, 75
anxiety 17, 19, 25, 31, 36, 62,
    75–6, 83, 90, 100–1
asphyxiation 11
awareness 102, 103

barbiturates 42–3
barriers to getting help 87–8
bereavement services 86–94
betrayal 14, 50
blame 27, 62, 69, 74–9 *see also*
    guilt
body, the 10–13
body dimorphic disorder 30–1
breaking the news 16
bullying 19, 31, 34
burning 17, 43

cancer 22

carbon monoxide poisoning 16,
    42–3
children 27–36; Childline 36;
    children's grief 81–4; child
    survivors 12, 64–6
clergy 86, 88
Compassionate Friends, The 93
conflict 33
coroner 1, 11, 47–9
counselling 90–2; British
    Association for Counselling &
    Psychotherapy 91
Cruse Bereavement Care 93
crying 74–5, 83, 89–90

deliberate self-harm 2, 27–8
denial 13–17, 73
depression 2, 5, 15–16, 19, 21,
    24–6, 28, 31, 35, 39, 62, 66, 68,
    71–5, 84
diabetes mellitus 22
doctor 86
drowning 11, 42, 68, 77
drug misuse 3, 22–3, 29–30, 33, 35,
    39, 61

emotional pain 2, 4
escaping pain 15, 18, 38
estate 55–7
euthanasia 6 *see also* physician
    assisted suicide
evidence 13
exams 31–2

executor 55–6

failure 31–2, 62
family 27, 54, 59, 70, 82–4; history
    21, 37; influence 33
fear 60, 74–6, 83
forgiveness 78–9
funeral 17, 51–5, 58; children and
    53–4; directors 52, 53; flowers
    53; gathering 54

gay & lesbian identity 23; partners
    41–2, 69–70
gender 20
grief, symptoms 12–13, 73–84;
    unresolved 80–2
guilt 4, 27, 61–78, 89, 91–2

hanging 12, 34, 38, 42, 44, 53, 89
healing and recovery 64, 72–3,
    75–95
hindsight 44–5, 71
HIV/AIDS 70
homelessness 19, 23, 39
hopelessness 22, 25–6, 38–40, 75
Huntington's chorea 22

idealization 33, 67–8, 79–80
inheritance 56–7
inquest 41, 48–51, 57
insomnia 11, 74
isolation 70

jumping 13, 33–4, 42, 44, 62

legislation 7, 43, 48
letting go 45–6
life insurance 57
loneliness 67–8, 76

losing: child 10–12, 29–30, 33,
    61–4; client 71–2; friend 71;
    grandparent 12; parent 5–6, 12,
    41, 53–4, 64–7, 88; sibling 9,
    12, 41, 67–8, 89, 92; spouse/
    partner 5, 10, 16, 41, 68–70,
    77–8
loss 22; history of 96–8

manipulation 4
martyr 4
media 10, 29, 33, 77
medication 6, 75 see also
    antidepressants
meditation 100–1
mental illness 21–3, 33, 39, 42, 50,
    60 see also depression/
    schizophrenia
motives 1, 4, 5, 7, 14, 24, 41, 70,
    73
motor neurone disease 22
mourning see grief
multiple sclerosis 22
murder-suicide 24

numbness 11

occupation 18; farmers 18, 24
offending behaviour 19, 32
open verdict 1, 49
overdose 4, 10–11, 20, 28, 31,
    42–3, 67, 77, 91

pain 5–6, 10, 79, 81
painkillers 14; paracetamol 31, 43
parents 6, 27–30, 55, 61–4
physical illness 5, 22, 25–6, 38–9,
    50, 60
planning the future 101–4

poisoning 42 *see also* overdose
police 47
post-mortem 11, 47–8
post trauma stress disorder 12
preoccupation with death 35, 74, 80
prevention 24–5, 43
previous attempts 24, 60
prisoners 23, 34–5

race 20
regret 44–5
rejection 14, 68
relationship difficulties 19, 32, 35, 78
relaxation 100–1
religious belief 7; and funerals 51–2
responsibility 4, 10, 44–5, 72–9
risk factors 1, 18–26, 66; in youth 27–36

sadness 10, 60
Samaritans, The 15, 23, 26
schizophrenia 21 *see also* mental illness
seasonal affective disorder (SAD) 21
self-esteem 19, 23, 31, 35
self-harm 1, 2, 27–8
self-help groups 89–90
self-image 30–1
shame *see* guilt
shock 11, 41, 66, 74, 76
shooting 9, 11, 24, 42
slashing wrists 10–11
social isolation 20
solicitor 56

sources of help 86–94
special occasions 92–3
stabbing 43
stress 3, 12, 18–19, 25–6, 31, 36, 75, 100–1
suicide: Act 1961 7; attempted 1, 2, 27, 33, 36 *see also* self-harm; attitudes 6–7; completed 2, 20; contagious 33–4; failed 43–4; impulsive 42; mass 4; method 20, 23, 42–3; myths 14–16; non-conventional 5; note 3, 15, 40, 42, 55; pact 6; physician assisted 6; planned 42; rational 5; rates 1, 19–20, 27
support 25, 85–94
survivors 1, 44, 59–81; needs of 85
Survivors of Bereavement by Suicide (SOBS) 93–4

tranquillizers 14, 43
truancy 35

vulnerability 15, 18–26, 35, 62

understanding 36–46, 66, 78
unemployment 19, 39

warning signs 44–5; in youth 35–6
websites 90–1
witness to the act 9, 12, 80–1
Worden, William 79–80
World Health Organization 1

youth 27–36
Yukiko, Okada 33–4